VOGUE® KNITTING
KNITS FOR PETS

VOGUE® KNITTING

KNITS FOR PETS

SIXTH&SPRING BOOKS
NEW YORK

SIXTH&SPRING BOOKS
233 Spring Street
New York, New York 10013

Library of Congress Cataloging-in-Publication Data

Library of Congress Control Number: 2006924841

ISBN: 1-933027-04-5
ISBN-13: 978-1-933027-04-3

Manufactured in China

1 3 5 7 9 10 8 6 4 2

First Edition

TABLE OF CONTENTS

INTRODUCTION

There's no better way to show off your creativity than putting something special and handmade on your beloved dog or cat, especially if your creation keeps the winter winds away! This book features an abundance of delightfully playful knit designs for your lovable furry friend, along with an assortment of cat-and dog-themed knits that make perfect gifts for the young people and animal lovers in your life.

Knitters at skill levels from beginner to advanced will enjoy the variety of patterns and stitches in *Knits for Pets*. Your two-legged friends will enjoy a fetching puppy purse, a winsomely droopy dog-eared knit hat, and several interactive projects for your dog or cat (you knit them, they munch on them or go crazy with their paws). There's also a laugh-out-loud-funny knit parody of one of today's most popular designer purses—with a dog theme, of course.

Your canine or feline companion will appreciate stylishly fun creations including a super-soft cat collar, a number of cozy beds for dogs and cats, and several sweaters to keep the cold at bay. Your pets will be grateful for the extra warmth and attention from the people and animals in their lives!

Knits for Pets includes easy-to-read instructions and diagrams along with a useful list of what kinds of yarn to use and how to get them. Pick a project, pull out your needles and get ready to **KNIT ON THE GO** all year long!

THE BASICS

What better way to show your canine and/or feline companions that you care—knit them a gift. For the knitter, the rewarding experience of creating a gift for a furry friend provides a unique opportunity to explore and experiment with various stitches, techniques, and yarns, all on a small scale. A practical yet pretty Dog Bag (page 21) uses a sturdy slip stitch pattern, and the fun furry trim adds a little panache. Practice your colorwork skills by making the Fair Isle Sweater (page 32) to keep your pooch warm during winter walks. Decorate your pet's room with the whimsical Pet Pillows (page 51).

This book combines fun function with creative designs for pets. The variety of skill levels from novice to expert, the simple and concise instructions, and the portability of these designs make this assortment of projects uniquely *Vogue Knitting On the Go!*

SIZING

The garments in this book are written for small, medium and large sized dogs. Take the basic measurements of your dog, such as width around body, length from neck to tail, and length from neck to legs before deciding which size to make. If your size is not given, you will have to do some math to adjust the numbers. Read the pattern through carefully before knitting

to determine where you will have to change the pattern. Be sure that you are getting the stated gauge, then multiply the stitch gauge by the finished body measurement, adding a few stitches if necessary to accommodate any stitch multiple. Adjust any length measurements based on the measurements of your pet.

YARN SELECTION

For an exact reproduction of the projects photographed, use the yarn listed in the "Materials" section of the pattern. We've chosen yarns that are readily available in the U.S. and Canada at the time of printing. The Resources list on pages 94 and 95 provides addresses of yarn distributors. Contact them for the name of a retailer in your area.

YARN SUBSTITUTION

You may wish to substitute yarns. Perhaps you view small-scale projects as a chance to incorporate leftovers from your yarn stash, or the yarn specified may not be available in your area. You'll need to knit to the given gauge to obtain the knitted measurements with a substitute yarn (see "Gauge" on page 11). Be sure to consider how the fiber content of the substitute yarn will affect the comfort and the ease of care of your projects.

To facilitate yarn substitution, *Vogue Knitting* grades yarn by the standard stitch gauge obtained in stockinette stitch. You'll

GAUGE

It is always important to knit a gauge swatch, and it is even more so with garments to ensure proper fit.

Patterns usually state gauge over a 4"/10cm span; however, it's beneficial to make a larger test swatch. This gives a more precise stitch gauge, a better idea of the appearance and drape of the knitted fabric, and a chance for you to familiarize yourself with the stitch pattern.

The type of needles used—straight or double-pointed, wood or metal—will influence gauge, so knit your swatch with the needles you plan to use for the project. Measure gauge as illustrated. Try different needle sizes until your sample measures the required number of stitches and rows. *To get fewer stitches to the inch/cm, use larger needles; to get more stitches to the inch/cm, use smaller needles.*

Knitting in the round may tighten the gauge, so if you measured the gauge on a flat swatch, take another gauge reading after you begin knitting. When the piece measures at least 2"/5cm, lay it flat and measure over the stitches in the center of the piece, as the side stitches may be distorted.

It's a good idea to keep your gauge swatch in order to test blocking and cleaning methods.

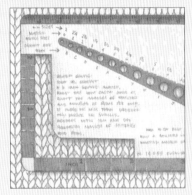

find a grading number in the "Materials" section of the pattern, immediately following the fiber type of the yarn. Look for a substitute yarn that falls into the same category. The suggested needle size and gauge on the yarn label should be comparable to that on the "Standard Yarn Weight" chart (see page 17).

After you've successfully gauge-swatched a substitute yarn, you'll need to figure out how much of the substitute yarn the project requires. First, find the total length of the original yarn in the pattern (multiply number of balls by yards/meters per ball). Divide this figure by the new yards/meters per ball (listed on the yarn label). Round up to the next whole number. The answer is the number of balls required.

FOLLOWING CHARTS

Charts are a convenient way to follow colorwork, lace, cable, and other stitch patterns at a glance. *Vogue Knitting* stitch charts utilize the universal knitting language of "symbolcraft." When knitting back and forth in rows, read charts from right to left on right side (RS) rows and from left to right on wrong side (WS) rows, repeating any stitch and row repeats as directed in the pattern. When knitting in the round, read charts from right to left on every round. Posting a self-adhesive note under your working row is an easy way to keep track of your place on a chart.

Two main types of colorwork are explored in this book: intarsia and stranding

Intarsia

Intarsia is accomplished with separate bobbins of individual colors. This method is ideal for large blocks of color or for motifs that aren't repeated close together. When changing colors, always pick up the new color and wrap it around the old color to prevent holes.

Stranding

When motifs are closely placed, colorwork is accomplished by stranding along two or more colors per row, creating floats on the wrong side of the fabric. This technique is sometimes called Fair Isle knitting after the traditional Fair Isle patterns that are composed of small motifs with frequent color changes.

To keep an even tension and prevent holes while knitting, pick up yarns alternately over and under one another across or around. While knitting, stretch the stitches on the needle slightly wider than the length of the float at the back to keep work from puckering.

When changing colors at the beginning of rows or rounds, carry yarn along for a few rows only, or cut yarn and rejoin when needed. It is important to keep the floats small and neat so they don't catch on paws or claws when the garment is pulled on.

BLOCKING

Blocking is a crucial finishing step in the knitting process. It is the best way to shape pattern pieces and smooth knitted edges in preparation for sewing together. Most garments retain their shape if the blocking stages in the instructions are followed carefully. Choose a blocking method according to the instructions on the yarn care label, and when in doubt, test-block your gauge swatch.

Wet Block Method

Using rust-proof pins, pin pieces to measurements on a flat surface and lightly dampen using a spray bottle. Allow to dry before removing pins.

Steam Block Method

With wrong sides facing, pin pieces. Steam lightly, holding the iron 2"/5cm above the knitting. Do not press or it will flatten stitches.

FINISHING

The pieces in this book use a variety of finishing techniques, from crocheting around the edges to embroidery. Also refer to the illustrations provided for other useful techniques: knitting with double-pointed needles, joining in the round, and embroidery stitches.

CARE

Refer to the yarn label for the recommended cleaning method. Many of the projects in the book can be either

STEM STITCH

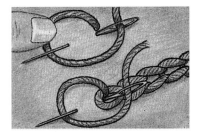

BLANKET STITCH

BACK STITCH

CHAIN STITCH

DUPLICATE STITCH

Duplicate stitch covers a knit stitch. Bring the needle up below the stitch to be worked. Insert the needle under both loops one row above and pull it through. Insert it back into the stitch below and through the center of the next stitch in one motion, as shown.

washed by hand, or in the machine on a gentle or wool cycle, using lukewarm water with a mild detergent. Do not agitate or soak for more than 10 minutes. Rinse gently with tepid water, then fold in a towel and gently press out the water. Lay flat to dry, away from excess heat and light. Check the yarn label for any specific care instructions such as dry cleaning or tumble drying.

POMPOMS

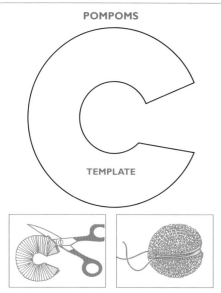

TEMPLATE

1 Following the template, cut two circular pieces of cardboard.

2 Hold the two circles together and wrap the yarn tightly around the cardboard several times. Secure and carefully cut the yarn.

3 Tie a piece of yarn tightly between the two circles. Remove the cardboard and trim the pompom to the desired size.

CIRCULAR NEEDLES

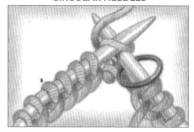

1 Hold the needle tip with the last cast-on stitch in your right hand and the tip with the first cast-on stitch in your left hand. Knit the first cast-on stitch, pulling the yarn tight to avoid a gap.

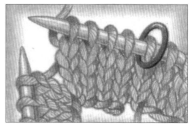

2 Work until you reach the marker. This completes the first round. Slip the marker to the right needle and work the next round.

TWISTED CORD

1 If you have someone to help you, insert a pencil or knitting needle through each end of the strands. If not, place one end over a doorknob and put a pencil through the other end. Turn the strands clockwise until they are tightly twisted.

2 Keeping the strands taut, fold the piece in half. Remove the pencils and allow the cords to twist onto themselves.

DOUBLE-POINTED NEEDLES

I Cast on the required number of stitches on the first needle, plus one extra. Slip this extra stitch to the next needle as shown. Continue in this way, casting on the required number of stitches on the last needle.

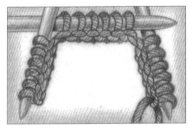

2 Arrange the needles as shown, with the cast-on edge facing the center of the triangle (or square).

3 Place a stitch marker after the last cast-on stitch. With the free needle, knit the first cast-on stitch, pulling the yarn tightly. Continue knitting in rounds, slipping the marker before beginning each round.

I With RS placed together, hold pieces on two parallel needles. Insert a third needle knitwise into the first stitch of each needle, and wrap the yarn around the needle as if to knit.

2 Knit these two stitches together, and slip them off the needles. *Knit the next two stitches together in the same manner.

3 Slip the first stitch on the third needle over the second stitch and off the needle. Repeat from the * in Step 2 across the row until all stitches have been bound off.

KNITTING TERMS AND ABBREVIATIONS

approx approximately

beg begin(ning)

bind off Used to finish an edge and keep stitches from unraveling. Lift the first stitch over the second, the second over the third, etc. (UK: cast off)

cast on A foundation row of stitches placed on the needle in order to begin knitting.

CC contrast color

ch chain(s)

cm centimeter(s)

cn cable needle

cont continu(e)(ing)

dc double crochet (UK: tr–treble)

dec decrease(ing)—Reduce the stitches in a row (knit 2 together).

dpn double pointed needle(s)

foll follow(s)(ing)

g gram(s)

garter stitch Knit every row. Circular knitting: Knit one round, then purl one round.

hdc half-double crochet (UK: htr–half treble)

inc increase(ing)—Add stitches in a row (knit into the front and back of a stitch).

k knit

k f & b knit into front and back of stitch

k2tog knit 2 stitches together

lp(s) loops(s)

LH left-hand

m meter(s)

M1 make one stitch—With the needle tip, lift the strand between last stitch worked and next stitch on the left-hand needle and knit into the back of it. One stitch has been added.

MC main color

mm millimeter(s)

oz ounce(s)

p purl

p2tog purl 2 stitches together

pat pattern

pick up and knit (purl) Knit (or purl) into the loops along an edge.

pm place marker—Place or attach a loop of contrast yarn or purchased stitch marker as indicated.

psso pass slip stitch over

rem remain(s)(ing)

rep repeat

rev St st reverse Stockinette stitch—Purl right-side rows, knit wrong-side rows. Circular knitting: Purl all rounds. (UK: reverse stocking stitch)

rnd(s) round(s)

RH right-hand

RS right side(s)

sc single crochet (UK: dc–double crochet)

sk skip

SKP Slip 1, knit 1, pass slip stitch over knit 1.

SK2P Slip 1, knit 2 together, pass slip stitch over k2tog.

sl slip—An unworked stitch made by passing a stitch from the left-hand to the right-hand needle as if to purl.

sl st slip stitch (UK: single crochet)

ssk slip, slip, knit—Slip next 2 stitches knitwise, one at a time, to right-hand needle. Insert tip of left-hand needle into fronts of these stitches from left to right. Knit them together. One stitch has been decreased.

st(s) stitch(es)

St st Stockinette stitch—Knit right-side rows, purl wrong-side rows. Circular knitting: Knit all rounds. (UK: stocking stitch)

tbl through back of loop

tog together

tr treble crochet (UK: dtr-double treble)

WS wrong side(s)

w&t wrap and turn

wyif with yarn in front

wyib with yarn in back

work even Continue in pattern without increasing or decreasing. (UK: work straight)

yd yard(s)

yo yarn over—Make a new stitch by wrapping the yarn over the right-hand needle. (UK: yfwd, yon, yrn)

* Repeat directions following * as many times as indicated.

[ ] Repeat directions inside brackets as many times as indicated.

Categories of yarn, gauge ranges, and recommended needle and hook sizes

Yarn Weight Symbol & Category Names	1 Super Fine	2 Fine	3 Light	4 Medium	5 Bulky	6 Super Bulky
Type of Yarns in Category	Sock, Fingering, Baby	Sport, Baby	DK, Light Worsted	Worsted, Afghan, Aran	Chunky, Craft, Rug	Bulky, Roving
Knit Gauge* in Stockinette Stitch to 4 Inches	27–32 sts	23–26 sts	21–24 sts	16–20 sts	12–15 sts	6–11 sts
Recommended Needle in Metric Size Range	2.25–3.25 mm	3.25–3.75 mm	3.75–4.5 mm	4.5–5.5 mm	5.5–8 mm	8 mm and larger
Recommended Needle U.S. Size Range	1 to 3	3 to 5	5 to 7	7 to 9	9 to 11	11 and larger
Crochet Gauge* Ranges in Single Crochet To 4 Inch	21–32 sts	16–20 sts	12–17 sts	11–14 sts	8–11 sts	5–9 sts
Recommended Hook in Metric Size Range	2.25–3.5 mm	3.5–4.5 mm	4.5–5.5 mm	5.5–6.5 mm	6.5–9 mm	9 mm and larger
Recommended Hook U.S. Size Range	B–1 to E–4	E–4 to 7	7 to I–9	I–9 to K–10½	K–10½ to M–13	M–13 and larger

*Guidelines only: The above reflects the most commonly used needle or hook sizes for specific yarn categories.

SKILL LEVELS FOR KNITTING

■□□□
Beginner
Ideal first project.

■■■□
Intermediate
For knitters with some experience. More intricate stitches, shaping and finishing.

■■□□
Very Easy Very Vogue
Basic stitches, minimal shaping, simple finishing.

■■■■
Experienced
For knitters able to work patterns with complicated shaping and finishing.

Hot diggity dog!

A delightfully entertaining design by Kate Jackson, this toy is the perfect size for your canine companion.

KNITTED MEASUREMENTS
■ Approx 10½"/26.5cm long x 10½"/26.5cm in diameter

MATERIALS
■ 1 3½oz/100g ball (each approx 190yd/174m) of Brown Sheep *Lamb's Pride Worsted* (wool/mohair) each in #M81 red baron for hot dog (A), #M140 aran for inner bun (B), #M08 wild oak for outer bun (C), #M155 lemon drop for mustard, #M180 ruby red for ketchup and #M120 limeade for green relish (4)
■ One pair size 10½ (6.5mm) needles *or size to obtain gauge*
■ Spare needle in smaller size
■ Tapestry needle
■ Polyester fiberfill for stuffing

GAUGE
16 sts and 20 rows to 4"/10cm over St st using size 10½ (6.5mm) needles.
Take time to check gauge.

HOT DOG

With A, cast on 45 sts.

Work in St st for 5½"/14cm, end with a WS row.

With spare needle, pick up 45 sts along cast-on edge.

Line up the 2 needles with WS together.

K 1 st from front needle and 1 st from back needle together across the row to join the hot dog into a tube.

Inner bun

Change to B and beg with a p row, work in St st for 3"/7.5cm, end with a WS row.

Outer bun

Change to C.

Row 1 K1, [kf&b of st] twice, k to last 3 sts, [kf&b of st] twice, k1—49 sts.

Row 2 and all even rows Purl.

Row 3 K3, kf&b of st, k to last 4 sts, kf&b of st, k3—51 sts.

Row 5 K4, kf&b of st, k to last 5 sts, kf&b of st, k4—53 sts.

Row 7 K5, kf&b of st, k to last 6 sts, kf&b of st, k5—55 sts.

Rows 9, 11 and 13 Knit.

Row 15 K4, k2tog, k to last 6 sts, k2tog, k4—53 sts.

Row 17 K3, k2tog, k to last 5 sts, k2tog, k3—51 sts.

Row 19 K2, k2tog, k to last 4 sts, k2tog, k2—49 sts.

Row 21 [K2tog] twice, k to last 4 sts, [k2tog] twice—45 sts.

Row 22 Purl.

Rep Rows 1–21 once more.

Rep inner bun. Bind off.

FINISHING

Sew one end of the hot dog closed by threading yarn needle with A through the last st of every row and pulling tightly. Leave the other end open for stuffing. Sew the ends of the bun together with C, attaching the outer bun to the hot dog between the inner bun sections. Sew the bound-off edge of the inner bun to the hot dog leaving a 3"/7.5cm gap in center for stuffing the bun later. Weave in any loose ends. Felt the hot dog to a finished size of about 10½"/26.5cm long. While still wet, stuff the toy firmly with fiberfill. If desired, you can put small squeaky toys or bells in the toy. Sew up the other end of the hot dog. sew the bun to hot dog seam and let the toy air dry. Embroider ketchup, mustard and relish on the toy using red, yellow and green yarn in the space between hot dog and inner bun.

DOG BAG
Kate spayed

Linda Cyr's gleeful spoof of the designer handbag du jour can be made at a fraction of the price of the original!

KNITTED MEASUREMENTS
▨ 12 x 8½ x 4"/30.5 x 21.5 x 10cm

MATERIALS
▨ 6 1¾oz/50g balls (each approx 56yd/52m) Karabella *Aurora Bulky* (wool) in #4 blue (MC) ⑤

▨ 1 1¾oz/50g ball (each approx 51yd/47m) Karabella *Barbados* (nylon/polyester) in #432 lavender (CC) ⑤

▨ Size 9 (5.5mm) circular needle, 24"/61cm long *or size to obtain gauge*
▨ Stitch marker
▨ ½yd/.5m lining material
▨ 3 sheets plastic needlepoint canvas
▨ 1 pair 22"/56cm long leather straps
▨ 1¼"/63mm toggle button
▨ Sewing needle
▨ Sewing thread
▨ Tapestry needle

GAUGE
20 sts and 40 rows to 4"/10cm over flat pat st using 9 (5.5 mm) needle.
Take time to check gauge.

PATTERN STITCH

Flat Pattern
(multiple of 4 sts plus 3)

Row 1(RS) *K3, sl 1 wyib; rep from * across, end k3.

Row 2 *K3, sl 1 wyif; rep from * across, end k3.

Row 3 K1, *sl 1 wyib, k3; rep from * across, end k1.

Row 4 K1, *sl 1 wyif, k3; rep from * across, end k1.

Rep rows 1–4 for flat pat.

Circular Pattern
(multiple of 4 sts)

Rnd 1 *K3, sl 1 wyib; rep from * around.

Rnd 2 *P3, sl 1 wyib; rep from * around.

Rnd 3 K1, *sl 1 wyib, k3; rep from * around, end k2.

Rnd 4 P1, *sl 1 wyib, p3; rep from * around, end p2.

Rep rnds 1–4 for circular pat.

BAG

Base
With MC, cast on 59 sts.
Work back and forth in flat pat for 40 rows.

Sides
Change to CC. Pick up and k 59 sts along each long edge of base and 23 sts along each short edge—164 sts. Join and pm for beg of rnds. P 3 rnds.

Change to MC. K 1 rnd.

Work in circular pat for 47 rnds.

Next rnd Work 87 sts in pat, bind off 23 sts, finish rnd—141 sts.

Rejoin yarn and beg working back and forth in flat pat, dec 1 st at each end of next 20 rows—101 sts.

Change to CC and beg working in rnds.

Next rnd K101 across top of bag, pick up and k 24 sts along diagonal edge, 23 sts along flat edge and 24 sts along diagonal edge—172 sts. Join and pm for beg of rnds. K 3 rnds. Bind off.

FLAP

With MC, cast on 15 sts.

Rows 1–52 Work in flat pat.

Row 53 K3, sl 1 wyib, k3, bind off 1 st, k2, sl 1 wyib, k3.

Row 54 K3, sl 1 wyif, k3, cast on 1 st, k3, sl 1 wyif, k3. Work 2 rows even.

Dec 1 st each end of next 6 rows—3 sts.

Next row Sl 1, k2tog, psso. Fasten off.

FINISHING

Cut plastic canvas for liner as follows:

Base 12 x 4"/30.5 x 10cm

Sides (make 2) 12 x 8"/30.5 x 20.5cm, measure in 4"/10cm along long side and 3"/7.5cm along short side, then cut off diagonal piece to match bag.

Short side 5½ x 4"/12.5 x 10cm

Tall side 8½ x 4"/21.5 x 10cm

Using needle and strong thread, lace edges together to form bag liner.

Cut fabric pieces to match plastic pieces adding a ½"/1.25cm seam allowance all around.

Sew fabric liner together with a ½"/1.25cm seam allowance, turn down ½"/1.25cm at top edges.

Insert fabric liner into plastic liner. With needle and thread, tack fabric liner to plastic liner at base corners. Insert liner into knitted bag. Fold top of fabric edge over plastic at top edge.

With needle and thread, sew top folded edge to knitted bag at base of CC band.

Fold CC band to outside, sew in place.

Sew flap in place 1"/2.5cm down from top edge of bag. Sew button under buttonhole.

Sew straps in place through all thickness 2½"/6.5cm down from top edge, ¼"/.6cm to each side of flap.

Pinch top corners together along tall side, sew in place.

Dog power

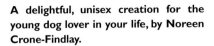

A delightful, unisex creation for the young dog lover in your life, by Noreen Crone-Findlay.

SIZE
Instructions are written for Children's size Medium.

KNITTED MEASUREMENTS
■ 18"/45.5cm circumference

MATERIALS
■ 1 1¾oz/50g ball (each approx 110yd/100m) of Dale of Norway *Heilo* (wool) each in #4203 light pink (A), #4516 dark pink (B) and #3152 brown (C) ③
■ One set (4) size 5 (3.75mm) double-pointed needles (dpn) *or size to obtain gauge*
■ Stitch marker

GAUGE
22 sts and 32 rows to 4"/10cm over St st using size 5 (3.75mm) dpn.
Take time to check gauge.

Note
Cuff of hat is knitted in the round and will roll naturally.

HAT
With A, cast on 23 sts on each of 4 dpns —92 sts. Join and pm for beg of rnds.
Rnds 1–30 Knit.
Cut A, join B.
Rnds 31–45 Knit.
Rnd 46 K23 (1st needle); ssk, k to last 2 sts on 2nd needle, k2tog (decs worked on 2nd needle); k23 (3rd needle); ssk, k to last 2 sts on 4th needle, k2tog (decs worked on 4th needle)—88 sts.
Rnd 47 Knit.
Rnds 48–59 Rep rnds 46 and 47. (On rnd 59 end with 23 sts on 1st needle, 9 sts on 2nd needle, 23 sts on 3rd needle, 9 sts on 4th needle—64 sts.)
Top of hat
Note Work 23 sts on first needle only.
Rnds 60–69 Work even on 23 sts in St st. Cut yarn, leaving a 36"/91.5cm length of yarn for grafting. Graft 23 sts from 1st needle to 23 sts on 3rd needle.
Underside of first ear
Note Join A to 2nd needle.
Row 1 K9.
Row 2 P9.
Row 3 (P1, k1) in 1st st, k to last st, (k1, p1) in last st—11 sts.
Row 4 Purl.
Rows 5–12 Rep rows 3 and 4—19 sts.
Rows 13–34 Work in St st.
Row 35 Ssk, k to last 2 sts, k2tog—17 sts.
Row 36 Purl.
Rows 37–42 Rep rows 35 and 36.
Bind off 11 sts.
Upper side of ear
With C, pick up 9 sts along opening above A under ear. Rep rows 1–42 of underside of ear. Stitch upper ear to lower ear.
Rep for 2nd ear.

FINISHING
Lightly steam press ears. Do not press hat. Weave in all ends.

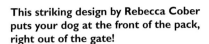

This striking design by Rebecca Cober puts your dog at the front of the pack, right out of the gate!

SIZE

Instructions are written for Dog's size Medium.

KNITTED MEASUREMENTS

▨ Chest 22"/56cm

MATERIALS

▨ 2 1¾oz/50g balls (each approx 137yd/125m) of Filatura Di Crosa/Tahki•Stacy Charles, Inc. *Zara* (wool) each in #1451 beige (A) and #1404 black (B) 🌑

▨ One pair each size 5 and 6 (3.75 and 4mm) needles *or size to obtain gauge*

▨ One set (4) size 5 (3.75mm) double-pointed needles (dpn)

▨ Size G/6 (4mm) crochet hook

GAUGE

24 sts and 26 rows to 4"/10cm over St st in chart pat using larger needles.
Take time to check gauge.

Note

When changing colors, twist yarns on WS to prevent holes.

SWEATER

Neck ribbing Using smaller needles and B, cast on 96 sts.

Row 1 (RS) *K2, p2; rep from * to end.

Row 2 (WS) *K2, p2; rep from * to end.

Rep these 2 rows for ribbing for 2"/5cm.

Chest shaping Change to larger needles. Using A, work 2 rows in St st.

Following chart rep rows 1–6 of chart pat, inc 1 st each side (working all incs sts in St st with A) on every RS row 6 times, then inc 1st each side on next 12 rows—132 sts.

Leg openings With A, work in St st across 16 sts, join second ball of A and bind off next 10 sts, continue in chart pat across next 80 sts keeping continuity of pat, join third ball of A and bind off 10 sts, with A work in St st across 16 sts. (**Note** The center section is worked in chart pat using A and B; the side sections are worked in St st using A.)

Work 3 sections of sweater separately using different balls for each section until leg openings measure 2"/5cm, ending with a WS row.

Join leg openings

Next row (RS) With A, k16, cast on 10 sts, cont in chart pat across next 80 sts, with A, cast on 10 sts, k to end of row—132 sts.

Cont as established until piece measures 9"/23cm from end of neck ribbing.

Back shaping Bind off 24 sts at the beg of next 2 rows—84 sts. Work 6 rows even in chart pat.

Next row (RS) Dec 1 st at each end of row—82 sts

Next row (WS) Work even in pat until end of row.

Rep last 2 rows 24 times. Bind off rem 34 sts.

Weave in ends. Block sweater. Sew center front seam, including neck ribbing

Leg ribbing With RS facing, using dpns and A, pick up and k 16 sts on each of 3 needles—48 sts. Join and pm for beg of rnds. Work in k2, p2 ribbing until legs measure 2"/5cm. Bind off in ribbing.

Body edging With crochet hook and A, start at beg of back shaping and work 1 row single crochet around the lower body, then with B work 1 row slip stitch.

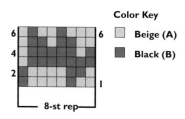

Color Key

☐ Beige (A)

■ Black (B)

6   6
4
2
          1

—8-st rep—

CAT MAT
Shed on this

■■■□

A cozy creation by Jenn Jarvis, this mat is a soft, comfortable place for your cat to spend 20 hours a day!

KNITTED MEASUREMENTS
■ 19 x 17"/48 x 43cm

MATERIALS
■ 2 1¾oz/50g balls (each approx 110yd/100m) of Lana Grossa//Unicorn Books & Crafts *Royal Tweed* (wool) in #37 magenta (A) (**5**)
■ 1 ball in #24 lime (B)
■ Size 7 (4.5mm) circular needle, 24"/61cm long *or size to obtain gauge*
■ Tapestry needle

GAUGE
16 sts and 23 rows to 4"/10cm over St st using size 7 (4.5mm) needle.
Take time to check gauge.

Notes

I Circular knitting needle is used to accommodate the large number of sts.
2 When changing colors, twist yarn on WS to prevent holes.

MAT

With B, cast on 80 sts. Work 5 rows in garter st.
Next row (RS) With B, k5; join A and k 70, add second ball of B, k5.
Next row (WS) With B, k5; with A, p70, with B, k5.
Rep last 2 rows 4 times more.
Next row (RS) With B, k5; with A, k18, beg chart with st 1 and work to st 34, with A, k18; with B, k5. Keeping 5 sts each side in garter st with B and rem sts in St st, cont as established to row 70.
Next row (RS) With B, k5; with A, k70 with B, k5.
Next row (WS) With B, k5; with A, p70; with B, k5.
Rep last 2 rows 4 times more.
With B, work in garter st for 5 rows.
Bind off. With A, embroider eye and tail lines in stem stitch.

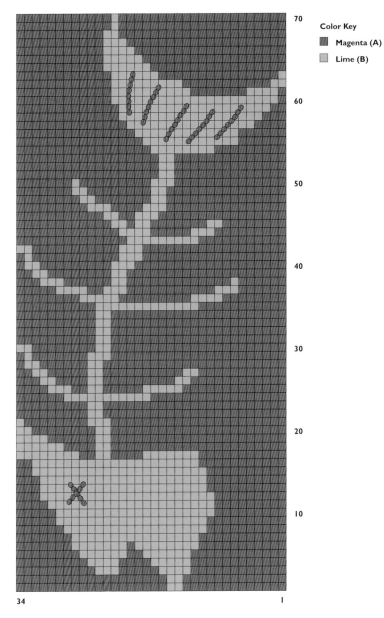

Color Key

■ Magenta (A)
□ Lime (B)

70

60

50

40

30

20

10

34

1

Bursting with color, this striking design by Jil Eaton makes your dog instantly recognizable from far away!

SIZES

Instructions are written for Dog's size Small (Medium, Large, X-Large.)

KNITTED MEASUREMENTS

■ Chest 13 (16, 24, 30)"/33 (40.5, 61, 76) cm

■ Length from neck to tail 11 (12, 15, 20)"/28 (30.5, 38, 51)cm

MATERIALS

■ 1 (1, 2, 2) 3oz/85g balls (each approx 197yd/180m) of Lion Brand *Wool-Ease* (wool/acrylic) each in #116 delft blue (A), #137 fuchsia (B), # 176 spring green (C) and #158 butter cup (D) (4)

■ One pair each sizes 8 and 9 (5 and 5.5mm) needles *or size to obtain gauge*

■ Size 8 (5mm) circular needle 16"/40cm long

■ One set (4) size 8 (5mm) double-pointed needles (dpn)

■ Stitch holders

■ Stitch marker

GAUGE

22 sts and 24 rows to 4"/10cm over St st and charted pat using larger needles.
Take time to check gauge.

BODY.

With smaller needles and A, cast on 57 (63, 95, 127) sts. Work in k1, p1 rib for 2 (2½, 3, 3)"/5 (6.5, 7.5, 7.5)cm, inc 15 (25, 37, 37) sts evenly spaced across last row—72 (88, 132, 164) sts. Change to larger needles and work in St st and chart pat (work 4-st rep 18 (22, 33, 41) times) until piece measures 3 (4, 6, 8)"/7.5 (10, 15, 20.5)cm from beg, end with a WS row. Cont in chart pat as foll:

DIVIDE FOR LEG OPENING

Next row (RS) Work 14 (15, 17, 21) sts, then place rem sts on a holder. Cont on these 14 (15, 17, 21) sts only for 2 (2½, 3, 4)"/5 (6.5, 7.5, 10)cm. Place sts on a 2nd holder. Cut yarn. Rejoin yarn and bind off next 8 (9, 10, 11) sts from first holder for leg opening, then work next 28 (40, 78, 100) sts only for 2 (2½, 3, 4)"/5 (6.5, 7.5, 10)cm, ending with a RS row. Place sts on a 3rd holder. Cut yarn. Rejoin yarn and bind off next 8 (9, 10, 11) sts from first holder for leg opening. Work rem 14 (15, 17, 21) sts for 2 (2½, 3, 4)"/5 (6.5, 7.5, 10) cm, ending with a RS row.

Next row (WS) Work 14 (15, 17, 21) sts on needle, cast on 8 (9, 10, 11) sts, then work 28 (40, 78, 100) sts from 3rd holder, cast on 8 (9, 10, 11) sts, then work rem 14 (15, 17, 21) sts from 2nd holder. Cont on all sts until piece measures 7 (8, 10, 14)"/18 (20.5, 25.5, 35.5)cm from beg.

SHAPE TAIL

Bind off 5 (5, 6, 7) sts at beg of next 2 (4, 6, 6) rows, dec 1 st each side every other row 6 (5, 6, 9) times, bind off 5 (5, 5, 7) sts at beg of next 4 rows, 0 (0, 6, 8) sts at beg of next 0 (0, 2, 2) rows. Bind off rem 30 (38, 52, 60) sts.

FINISHING

Block piece. Sew center seam from neck to beg of tail shaping.

TAIL BORDER

With RS facing, circular needle and A, pick up and k 68 (80, 124, 156) sts evenly around tail shaping. Join pm for beg of rnds. Work in k1, p1 rib for 1"/2.5cm. Bind off in rib.

LEG BORDER

With RS facing, dpn and A, pick up and k 36 (42, 50, 60) sts evenly around each leg opening. Join and pm for beg of rnds. Work in k1, p1 rib for 1"/2.5cm. Bind off in rib.

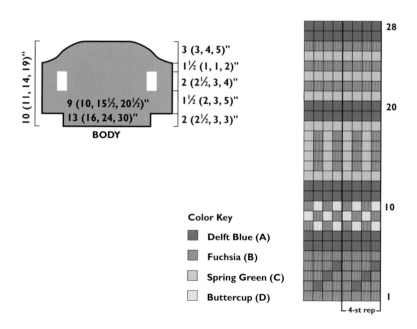

3 (3, 4, 5)"
1½ (1, 1, 2)"
2 (2½, 3, 4)"
1½ (2, 3, 5)"
2 (2½, 3, 3)"

10 (11, 14, 19)"

9 (10, 15½, 20½)"
13 (16, 24, 30)"

BODY

28
20
10
1

4-st rep

Color Key

Delft Blue (A)
Fuchsia (B)
Spring Green (C)
Buttercup (D)

Puppy purse

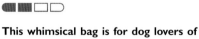

This whimsical bag is for dog lovers of all ages. Designed by Noreen Crone-Findlay.

KNITTED MEASUREMENTS
▨ Approx 9 x 12"/23 x 30.5cm

MATERIALS
▨ 2 4oz/125g balls (each approx 250yd/230m) of S. R. Kertzer *Super 10* (cotton) in #53 iron (MC) ▨
▨ 1 ball in #3768 jade (CC)
▨ One pair size 10 (6mm) needles *or size to obtain gauge*
▨ Stitch holder
▨ Wire coat hanger
▨ Heavy-duty wire cutters
▨ Safety glasses
▨ Heavy-duty needle nose pliers
▨ Sandpaper or file to smooth ends of coat hanger
▨ Three Quick Stick adhesive backed felt sheets in black (9x12"/23x30.5cm)
▨ Two tubs 12oz Mass O'Glass hand-crafted glass bead assortment

GAUGE
16 sts and 30 rows to 4"/10cm over garter stitch using size 10 (6mm) needles and 2 strands of yarn held together.
Take time to check gauge.

Notes

1 Bag is worked in garter stitch (knit all rows) with 2 strands of yarn held together for all sections.

2 When following charts, note that odd-numbered rows are read from right to left and even-numbered rows are read from left to right. Each box represents one stitch. Decreases are indicated by the line moving in one box (or more). Decrease at beginning of rows are worked "ssk" and "k2tog" at end of row. Increases are indicated by the line moving out one or more boxes. Increases at beginning of the row are worked (p1, k1) in first st. Increases at end of row are worked (k1, p1) in last st.

3 Safety Note When working with wire, wear safety glasses.

SIDES OF BAG
(make 2)
Beg with row 1 of chart 1, with 2 strands MC held tog, cast on 2 sts. Follow rows 1–14 of chart 1 in garter st, then cut yarn. Sl sts onto holder and set aside.

With 2 strands MC held tog, cast on 32 sts. Work rows 1–35 of chart 2 in garter st, casting on 1 st at end of row 35, then k sts from holder—37 sts.

Next row foll chart 2 row 36, k37 sts.

Tail Work rows 37–58 of chart 2, then bind off 3 sts at end of row 58.

Rejoin yarn and bind off 12 sts—18 sts rem.

Head Work rows 37–58 of chart 2 in garter st, then bind off 3 sts.
Rep for second side of bag.

BASE OF BAG

With 2 strand MC held tog, cast on 24 sts.
Follow chart 3 in garter st.
Bind off.

BLANKET – BAG FLAP

With 2 strands CC held tog, cast on 24 sts.
Follow chart 3 in garter st.
Bind off.

FINISHING

Weave yarn ends into WS of bag. Remove paper backing from Quick Stick felt. Lay body side on the felt starting at lower left-hand side for one side of bag and lower right-hand side for other. (Be careful that the sides of the bag are facing in opposite directions and not the same way.) Press down on the felt to adhere to the bag side. Trim away excess felt. Turn over sides and rub firmly to fully adhere the felt to the bag. Rep this process for the base of the bag. Stitch one ¼"/6mm black bead to each side of the head for eyes.

Wrap one strand of CC around your index finger 5 times and snip. Stitch the loops just above the eye for eyelashes. Snip loops open.

Stitch the sides of the bag tog from the base of the neck around the head to the lower edge of front and from the base of the tail around the tail to the lower edge of the back. Leave lower edges and top edge between tail and head open. Leave tip of tail and ear open for ends of handle. Stitch base to lower edges.

Stitch a black ½"/12mm bead to nose. Stitch a large bead to the tip of the hem of both sides of the blanket. Fold blanket in half and stitch around the edges on one side of the body. This forms a pocket for a cellphone or i-pod.

COLLAR

String beads onto yarn and tie around throat. Stitch through beads, anchoring to dog.

HANDLE

Wearing safety glasses, cut the hook off wire coat hanger and straighten the remaining wire. Cut a piece of wire about 18"/45.5cm long. Notch the wire at the 18"/45.5cm mark with a file to make it easier to twist off. With a nail file, file or sandpaper, sand the ends smooth. With the pliers, twist one end into a loop. Slide beads on the wire. Bend the wire into an arch shape. Bend the remaining end into a loop. Insert one loop inside ear and other loop inside tip of tail. Stitch in place.

chart 2

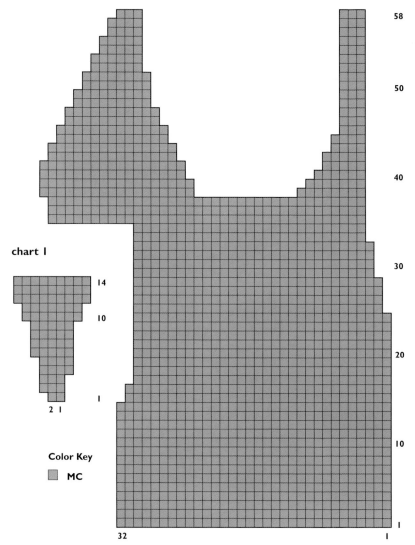

chart 1

58

50

40

30

14

10

20

1

2 1

10

Color Key

MC

1

32   1

chart 3

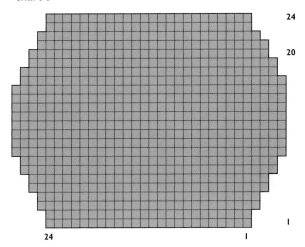

24

20

1

24

1

Color Key

 MC

DOG SWEATER
Glamour pup

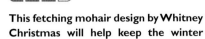

This fetching mohair design by Whitney Christmas will help keep the winter chill away.

SIZES

Instructions are written for Dog's size Small (Medium). Shown in size Small.

KNITTED MEASUREMENTS
▦ Chest 13 (18)"/33 (45.5)cm
▦ Length 10 (12)"/25 (30.5)cm

MATERIALS
▦ 2 (3) 1.75oz/50g skeins (each approx 87yd/80m) of Berroco *Optik* (cotton/acrylic/mohair/metallic/polyester) in #4944 cadaquez (A) ◪
▦ 2 (3) 1.75oz/50g balls (each approx 108yd/108m) of Berroco *Smart Mohair* (mohair/ acrylic/ polyester) in #8827 blue opal (B) ◪
▦ One pair size 10½ (6.5mm) needles *or size to obtain gauge*
▦ Tapestry needle

GAUGE

12 sts and 14 rows to 4"/10cm over St st using size 10½ needles and one strand each of A and B held tog.
Take time to check gauge.

BODY

With one strand each A and B held tog, cast on 30 (42) sts. Work in k1, p1 rib for 2"/5cm, end with a RS row.

Row 1 and all WS rows Purl.
Row 2 (RS) K2, M1, k to last 2 sts, M1, k2—32(44)sts.
Rows 3–16 Rep rows 1 and 2 six times more— 44 (56) sts . Work even in St st for 1"/2.5cm, end with a WS row.

Divide for legs
Next row (RS) K5 (7), join second ball of A and B and bind off 5 (7) sts, k to last 10 (14) sts, join third ball of A and B bind off 5 (7) sts, k to end. Work is now divided into three sections. Work each section separately in St st for 1½"/4cm, end with a WS row.

Body shaping
Next row (RS) K across first section, cast on 4 (6) sts, work across second section and cast on 4 (6) sts, k to end 42(54) sts. Continue working in St st until piece measures 8(10)"/20.5(25.5)cm. Work in k1, p1 rib for 2"/5cm. Bind off very loosely.

SLEEVES

With one strand each A and B held tog, cast on 16 (22) sts. Work in k1, p1 rib for 2"/5cm, end with a RS row. Work even in St st until piece measures 4½ (6)"/11.5 (15)cm from beg. Bind off loosely.

FINISHING

Block pieces. Sew sleeve seams. Sew sleeves into openings, centering seam toward inner back corner of opening. Sew center body seam to form tube.

This comfortable creation by Cecelia Madison is a great place for identification tags or anything else your cat needs to wear. Choose from two versions.

KNITTED MEASUREMENTS
- 22"/56cm (before felting)
- 14"/36cm (after felting)

MATERIALS
- 3½oz/100g ea approx. 223yds/205m Patons *Classic Merino Wool* (wool) in #77732 that's pink (A)
- 1¾oz/50g ea approx. 164yds/150m Patons *Silverlash* (polyester/lurex) in #81405 maroon magic (B)
- One set (4) size 11 (8mm) double-pointed needles (dpn) *or size to obtain gauge*
- Tapestry needle
- One size 2 snap
- Sewing needle
- Thread to match yarn

GAUGE

10 rows to 4"/10cm over I-cord using size 11 (8mm) dpn (before felting).
Take time to check gauge.

Note

This version of the collar is worked with 1 strand each of *Classic Merino Wool* (A) and *Silverlash* (B) held tog throughout.

COLLAR

With 1 strand each of A and B held tog, cast on 3 sts. Work I-cord for 22"/56cm as foll: K3, do not turn; slide sts to beg of needle, pull yarn across back and work again from the RS.

Last row K3tog; cut yarn and draw through rem st.

Work yarn ends from cast-on and bind-off into collar and trim excess.

Rub and shake the collar gently to pull the ends of the eyelash free from the knitting; this will prevent them from being matted into the wool during felting.

Felting

Put collar in zippered pillowcase. Add to washing machine with towels, jeans, or tennis balls for added friction. Use the lowest water level, the hottest water setting, and a small amount of soap. Set machine to agitate and check progress every 5–10 minutes. Reset the machine to agitate if more time is needed. Do not allow machine to enter spin cycle, as this will cause a permanent crease in the collar. When the wool is matted and there is no visible stitch definition, rinse collar. Roll it in a towel and squeeze out as much water as possible. Lay flat to dry.

FINISHING

Cut the collar close to one end. With sewing needle and thread, sew one part of the snap to the cut edge. Trim collar to desired length and sew the other part of the snap to the other end.

- 18½"/47cm (before felting).
- 14"/36cm (after felting).

MATERIALS
- 3½oz/100g ea approx. 223yds/205m Patons *Classic Merino Wool* (wool) in #77732 that's pink (A) (4)
- 1¾oz/50g ea approx. 164yds/150m Patons *Silverlash* (polyester/lurex) in #81405 maroon magic (B) (4)
- One set (4) size 11 (8mm) double-pointed needles (dpn) *or size to obtain gauge*
- Tapestry needle
- One size 2 snap
- Sewing needle
- Thread to match yarn

GAUGES
- 10 rows to 4"/10cm over I-cord using size 11 (8mm) dpn (before felting)
Take time to check gauge.

Note
This version of the collar is worked with 1 strand *Classic Merino Wool* (A) and 2 strands *Silverlash* (B) held tog throughout.

COLLAR
With 1 strand A and 2 strands B held tog, cast on 3 sts. Work I-cord for 18½"/47cm as foll: K3, do not turn; slide sts to beg of needle, pull yarn across back and work again from the RS.

Last row K3tog; cut yarn and draw through rem st.

Work yarn ends from cast-on and bind-off into collar and trim excess.

Rub and shake the collar gently to pull the ends of the eyelash free from the knitting; this will prevent them from being matted into the wool during felting.

Felting
Put collar in zippered pillowcase. Add to washing machine with towels, jeans, or tennis balls for added friction. Use the lowest water level, the hottest water setting, and a small amount of soap. Set machine to agitate and check progress every 5–10 minutes. Reset the machine to agitate if more time is needed. Do not allow machine to enter spin cycle, as this will cause a permanent crease in the collar. When the wool is matted and there is no visible stitch definition, rinse collar. Roll it in a towel and squeeze out as much water as possible. Lay flat to dry.

FINISHING
Cut the collar close to one end. With sewing needle and thread, sew one part of the snap to the cut edge. Trim collar to desired length and sew the other part of the snap to the other end.

This colorful pattern by Becky Billock makes your pooch stand out in the crowd.

SIZES

Instructions are written for Dog's size Small (Medium, Large, X-Large).

KNITTED MEASUREMENTS

■ Small 12½ x 4½"/31.5 x 11.5cm (without fringe)

■ Medium 23 x 8"/58.5 x 20.5cm (without fringe)

■ Large 33½ x 11½"/85 x 19cm (without fringe)

■ X-Large 44 x 15"/111.5 x 38cm (without fringe)

MATERIALS

■ 2 (2, 3, 3) 1¾oz/50g balls (each approx 115yd/105m) Jaeger Westminster Fibers *Aqua Cotton* DK (cotton) #320 deep (MC) ③

■ 1 (2, 2, 3) balls in #331 marigold (A)

■ 1 (2, 2, 2) balls in #330 daffodil (B)

■ 1 (1, 2, 2) balls in #332 india (C)

■ Size 10½ (6.5mm) circular knitting needle, 24"/61cm long (straight needles will do for smallest size) *or size to obtain gauge*

■ One set (4) size 11 (8mm) double-pointed needles (dpn)

■ Crochet hook size I/9 (5.5mm) for fringe

■ Four large snaps

GAUGE

12 sts and 18 rows to 4"/10cm over St st using 3 strands of yarn held tog and size 10½ (6.5 mm) needles.
Take time to check gauge.

Note

Use 3 strands of yarn held tog throughout

STRIPE SEQUENCE

Row 1 3 strands of MC.

Row 2 2 strands of MC, 1 strand of A.

Row 3 1 strand of MC, 2 strands of A.

Row 4 3 strands of A.

Row 5 2 strands of A, 1 strand of B.

Row 6 1 strand of A, 2 strands of B.

Rows 7—9 3 strands of B.

Row 10 2 strands of B, 1 strand of C.

Row 11 1 strand of B, 2 strands of C.

Rows 12 and 13 3 strands of C.

Row 14 2 strands of C, 1 strand of MC.

Row 15 1 strand of C, 2 strands of MC.

Row 16 3 strands of MC.

Rep rows 1–16 for stripe sequence.

PONCHO

With circular needle and 3 strands of MC held tog, cast 3 sts.

Note Work first row in MC, then continue in stripe sequence.

Row 1(RS) K1, yo, k1, yo, k1—5 sts.

Row 2 P1, yo, p to last st, yo, p1—7 sts.

Row 3 K1, yo, k to last st, yo, k1.

Row 4 P1, yo, p to last st, yo, p1.

Working in stripe sequence, rep rows 3 and 4, inc 1 st on each side *every* row for 16 (32, 48, 64) rows—43(75, 107, 139) sts. Continuing with MC only, work 4 rows in garter st.

Bind off all sts.

Weave in ends.

FRINGE

Using 11"/28cm lengths of yarn, and holding 4 strands tog for each fringe, attach fringe with crochet hook through yo spaces along the side edges of the poncho, using colors corresponding to the stripes.

STRAPS

With dpn and 3 strands of MC held tog, cast on 4 sts. Work a 4-st I-cord for 10 (20, 30, 40)"/25.5 (51, 76, 101.5)cm as foll: K4, do not turn; slide sts to beg of needle, pull yarn across back and work again from the RS. Cut yarn and draw through sts. Fasten off securely.

Note Strap length should be equal to the chest measurement of your dog. Work the second strap the same, using 3 strands of MC or one of the contrasting colors. Place both straps side by side lengthwise along bound off edge of poncho, lining up center of the straps with the center of the poncho. Attach straps to poncho for only 4"/10cm on either side of the center (not all the way to the fringe edge of poncho). Sew two pair of snaps to each strap.

This authentic Icelandic pattern by Védis Jónsdóttir evokes brisk afternoons, gorgeous blue skies, and fresh sea breezes.

SIZE

Instructions are written for Dog's size Small.

KNITTED MEASUREMENTS

- Body 14"/35.5cm
- Back 12"/30.5cm

MATERIALS

- 1 1¾oz/50g ball (each approx 105yd/97m) of JCA/Reynolds *Lite-Lopi* each in #0059 black (A), #3177 heathered green (B), #0443 blue (C), #0434 red (D) and #0051 cream (E) **(4)**
- One set (4) each size 4 and 7 (3.5 and 4.5mm) double-pointed needles (dpn) *or size to obtain gauge*
- Stitch holders
- Stitch marker

GAUGE

18 sts and 24 rows to 4"/10cm over St st and charted pat using larger needles.
Take time to check gauge.

Notes

1 Back is worked back and forth but body, sleeves and yoke are worked in the round.

2 Round of body begins at left side of body but on yoke at left side of back.

3 Measure dog's length and body before starting, adjusting sweater length if necessary.

4 When changing colors, twist yarn on WS to prevent holes.

BODY

With larger needles and A, cast on 33 sts. Work back and forth in k1, p1 rib for 3 rows.

Back (RS) P1, k1, p1, work St st on 27 sts, p1, k1, p1.

(WS) K1, p1, k1, work St st on 27 sts, k1, p1, k1.

Rep these 2 rows until back measures 5"/12.5cm from cast-on edge.

Body Cast on 27 sts, join to work in rnds —60 sts.

Next rnd Work St st on 33 back sts, work rib on 27 sts. Work in k1, p1 rib and St st as established for 2 more rnds, then work St st on all sts until body measures 1½"/4cm from lower body ribbing.

Next rnd K8, inc 1 st, k11, inc 1 st, k41 sts (back)—62 sts. Work even for ½"/2cm.

Next rnd K9, inc 1 st, k11 sts, inc 1 st, k42 sts—64 sts.

Work even (without further incs) until body measures 8½"/22cm from first cast-on edge (back). Set aside and work sleeves.

SLEEVES – FRONT LEGS

With larger needles and A, cast on 20 sts. Place marker for beg, join to work in rnds, being careful not to twist sts on needle. Work 3 rnds in k1, p1 rib. Work 1 rnd in St st, inc 4 sts evenly spaced—24 sts. Work until sleeve measures 2½"/7cm from cast-on edge. Sl 6 sts to one holder, sl rem 18 sts second holder. Work second sleeve in same manner.

YOKE

Join body and sleeves

With larger needles and A, k4 from body, sl 6 body sts to holder, k18 from first sleeve, k11 body sts for front, sl 6 body sts to holder, k18 from second sleeve, k37 body sts for back—88 sts. Follow color chart and dec as indicated on rnds 10, 16 and 20—55 sts. Change to smaller needles and A. K next rnd, dec 3 sts evenly—52 sts. Work 4 rnds in k1, p1 rib with A, 2 rnds with B, 1 rnd with D. Bind off loosely.

FINISHING

Sleeve Gusset

Using larger needles, pick up 6 sts from body holder. Work 6 rows St st (from RS). Graft to sleeve. Sew sides of gusset to body. (This is done to give the sweater more flexibility.) Work gusset under second sleeve.

Weave in all loose ends. Rinse sweater and lay flat to dry.

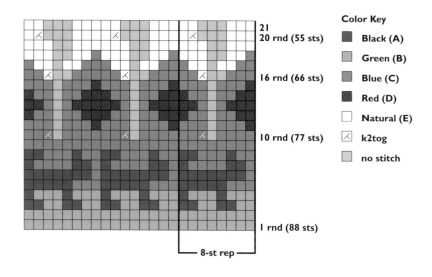

21
20 rnd (55 sts)
16 rnd (66 sts)
10 rnd (77 sts)
1 rnd (88 sts)

8-st rep

Color Key

■	Black (A)
▨	Green (B)
▨	Blue (C)
■	Red (D)
□	Natural (E)
⧄	k2tog
▨	no stitch

Gitta Schrade's whimsical, marvelously lifelike designs give a striking, decorative touch to any room.

KNITTED MEASUREMENTS
■ Approx 16"/40.5cm square

MATERIALS
■ 6 1¾oz/50g balls (each approx 109yd/100m) of Naturally NZ *Merino et Soie* 10-ply (wool/silk) in #105 green (MC) [4]
■ 1 1¾oz/50g ball (each approx 131yd/120m) of Naturally NZ *Sensation* (wool/angora) in #306 black (CC) [4]
■ Small amount grey yarn
■ One pair size 6 (4mm) needles, *or size to obtain gauge*
■ One set (4) size 6 (4mm) double-pointed needles (dpn)
■ Six stitch markers
■ Small amount polyester fiberfill
■ 16"/40.5cm square pillow form
■ 12"/30.5cm green zipper
■ Tapestry needle
■ One pair 1"/25mm cat eyes
■ Transparent fishing line for whiskers
■ One ⅜"/10mm-wide lightweight pet collar, or ribbon
■ Craft glue

GAUGE
20 sts and 26 rows to 4"/10cm over pat st using size 6 (4mm) needles.
Take time to check gauge.

PATTERN STITCH
Row 1 (RS) *K2, p2; rep from * to end.
Rows 2 and 4 K the knit sts; p the purl sts.
Row 3 *P2, k2; rep from * to end.
Rep rows 1–4 for pat st.

PILLOW COVER
With straight needles and MC, cast on 80 sts.
Front facing
Work in pat st for 8 rows.
Place a marker at beg and end of last row.
Front
Cont in pat st until piece measures 16"/40.5cm from markers, end with a WS row. Place a marker at beg and end of last row to mark folding point.
Back
Work even in pat st until piece measures 16"/40.5cm from 2nd markers, end with a WS row. Place a marker at beg and end of last row to mark folding point.
Back facing
Work even in pat st for 8 more rows. Bind off.

FINISHING
Fold pillow in half at center marker. Sew side seams between markers, omitting first and last 8 rows. Fold facing to inside.

Sew first and last 2"/5cm of opening. Position and sew zipper in place.

Notes for working chart

For RH decs, work SKP; for LH decs, work k2tog or p2tog. Work all decs 1 st in from edge. For incs, work M1 at 1 st in from edge for a smoother edge. When eliminating more than 2 sts at a time, bind off.

CAT

With straight needles and CC, cast on 44 sts. Work 82 rows of chart in St st, following chart for shaping. On row 61 of chart, work 16 sts, join 2nd ball of yarn, bind off 3 sts, work to end. Working both sides at once, complete chart.

SNOUT

With straight needles and CC, cast on 4 sts and work in St st as foll:

Row 1 (RS) K4, cast on 1 st.

Row 2 P5, cast on 1 st.

Rows 3–6 Cast on 1 st at end of each row—10 sts.

Row 7 (RS) K10.

Row 8 P8, p2tog—9 sts.

Row 9 K7, k2tog—8 sts.

Rows 10–13 Dec 1 st at end of each row—4 sts.

Row 14 (WS) P4.

Row 15 K4, do not turn.

Next Rnd Divide the following sts evenly over 3 dpn: sl 4 sts from needle to dpn, pick up and k 12 sts down side, 4 sts along cast-on edge, and 12 sts up 2nd side—32 sts. Join and pm for beg of rnds. Work even in St st for 5 rnds. Bind off loosely.

FINISHING

Open zipper. Center and pin cat applique on front of pillow, with lower edge of applique about 2"/5cm from zipper edge of pillow. Sew applique to pillow, leaving a small opening at each side of neck for tucking under collar edges. With grey yarn, embroider markings on snout as shown on chart. Cut six 7"/17.5cm lengths of fishing line and bundle them tog at the center with a rubber band. Pull the ends slightly so that they are uneven on each side. Cover rubber band with adhesive tape. Position center of whisker bundle inside nose and draw the ends of the whiskers through to the RS. Stuff nose lightly with fiberfill and sew nose to applique referring to chart for positioning. Attach eyes. Cut pet collar to size, allowing 1"/2.5cm at each end for tucking under applique. Use craft glue to adhere collar to applique; tuck ends underneath applique and glue in place. Or, glue ribbon in place for collar.

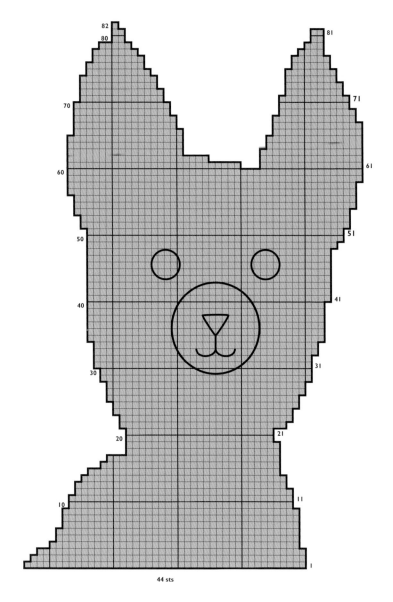

82
80
81
71
70
61
60
51
50
41
40
31
30
21
20
11
10
1

44 sts

■■ ■■ ■■ ▭

BLACK AND WHITE DOG PILLOW

KNITTED MEASUREMENTS
▨ Approx 16"/40.5cm

MATERIALS
▨ 6 1¾oz/50g balls (each approx 109yd/100m) of Naturally NZ *Merino et Soie* 10-ply (wool/silk) in #104 blue (MC) ▨

▨ 1 1¾oz/50g ball (each approx 131yd/120m) of Naturally NZ *Sensation* (wool/angora) each in #300 white (A) and #306 black (B) ▨

▨ One pair size 6 (4mm) needles, *or size to obtain gauge*

▨ One set (4) size 6 (4mm) double-pointed needles (dpn)

▨ Six stitch markers

▨ Small amount polyester fiberfill

▨ 16"/40.5cm square pillow form

▨ 12"/30.5cm zipper in blue

▨ Tapestry needle

▨ One pair ¾"/19mm dog's eyes

▨ One ½"/13mm-wide lightweight pet collar or 8"/20.5cm of ½"/6mm wide ribbon

▨ Craft glue

GAUGE
20 sts and 26 rows to 4"/10cm over pat st using size 6 (4mm) needles.
Take time to check gauge.

PILLOW COVER
Work as for black cat on page 52.

APPLIQUE
With straight needles and A, cast on 57 sts. Following notes to work chart as for black cat on page 53, work 85 rows of chart in St st, following chart for shaping and color changes.

SNOUT
With straight needles and B, cast on 5 sts.

Rows 1–4 Work even in St st.
Next rnd (RS) Divide the following sts evenly over 3 dpn: k1, SKP, k2, do not turn, sl these sts to dpn, pick up and k 3 sts down side, 5 sts along cast-on edge and 3 sts along 2nd side—14 sts. Join and pm for beg of rnds. Change to A and work even in St st for 3 rnds.
Next rnd K6, M1, k5, M1, k3—16 sts. Work even in St st for 2 rnds.
Next rnd K6, M1, k7, M1, k3—18 sts. Work even in St st for 2 rnds. Bind off loosely.

RIGHT EAR
Beg at base with straight needles and B, cast on 20 sts.

Row 1–8 Work even in St st.
Row 9 (RS) K1, k2tog, k to last 3 sts, SKP, k1—18 sts.
Row 10 P to last 3 sts, p2tog, p1—17 sts.
Row 11 K1, k2tog, k to end—16 sts.

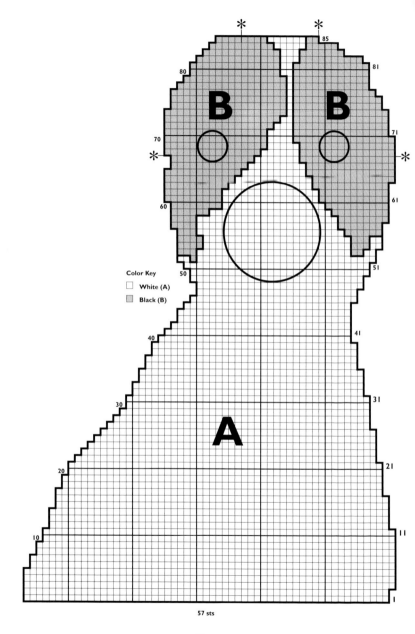

Color Key

☐ White (A)
▨ Black (B)

B **B**

A

57 sts

Rows 12 P to last 3 sts, p2tog, p1—15 sts.

Row 13–16 Rep rows 9–12—10 sts.

Row 17 K1, k2tog, k to last 3 sts, SKP, k1—8 sts

Row 18 Purl.

Rows 19–22 Rep rows 17 and 18 twice—4 sts.

Row 23 [K2tog] twice—2 sts.

Row 24 Purl.

Row 25 K2tog.

Fasten off. Mark center 8 sts at base of ear. Fold first marked st at left over to first marked st at right and sew the overlap in place along the base.

LEFT EAR

Work as for right ear, reversing all shaping and the overlapping at the base.

FINISHING

Open zipper. Center and pin dog applique on front of pillow, with lower edge of applique about ½"/1.3cm from zipper edge of pillow. Sew applique to pillow. Stuff snout lightly with fiberfill and sew to applique referring to chart for positioning. Sew base of ears between sts marked with * on chart. Attach eyes. Cut pet collar to size, allowing 1"/2.5cm at each end for tucking under applique. Use craft glue to adhere collar to applique. Tuck ends underneath applique and glue in place. Or, glue ribbon in place for collar.

BROWN DOG PILLOW

KNITTED MEASUREMENTS

▨ Approx 16"/40.5cm square

MATERIALS

▨ 6 1¾oz/50g balls (each approx 109yd/100m) of Naturally NZ *Merino et Soie* 10-ply (wool/silk) in #103 white (MC) [4]

▨ 1 1¾oz/50g ball (each approx 55yd/50m) of S.R. Kertzer, Ltd., *Baby Monkey* (or Naturally *Milan*) (polymide) in #16 brown (A) [4]

▨ 1 1¾oz/50g ball (each approx 77yd/70m) of S.R. Kertzer, Ltd., *Ranee* (or Naturally *Imagine*) (polymide/polyester) in #603 orange (B) [4]

▨ One pair size 6 (4mm) needles, *or size to obtain gauge*

▨ One set (4) size 6 (4mm) double-pointed needles (dpn)

▨ Six stitch markers

▨ Small amount polyester fiberfill

▨ 16"/40.5cm square pillow form

▨ 12"/30.5cm white zipper

▨ Tapestry needle

▨ One pair 1"/25mm dog eyes

▨ Small amount of ribbon for bow

GAUGE

20 sts and 6 rows to 4"/10cm over pat st using size 6 (4mm) needles.
Take time to check gauge.

PILLOW COVER

Work as for black cat on page 52.

APPLIQUE

With straight needles and A, cast on 51 sts. Following notes for working chart as for black cat on page 53, work 98 rows of chart in St st, following chart for shaping and color changes. On row 85 of chart, work 25 sts, join 2nd ball of yarn, bind off 9 sts, work to end. Working both sides at once, complete chart.

SNOUT

With straight needles and A, cast on 6 sts.
Rows 1–4 Work even in St st.
Row 5 (RS) K1, SKP, k2tog, k1—4 sts.
Row 6 Purl.
Row 7 SKP, k2tog—2 sts. Do not turn.
Next rnd (RS) Divide the following sts evenly over 3 dpn: sl 2 sts from needle to dpn, pick up and k 5 sts down side, 6 sts along cast-on edge and 5 sts along 2nd side—18 sts. Join and pm for beg of rnds. Change to B and work even in St st for 3 rnds.
Next rnd K5, M1, k6, M1, k to end—20 sts. Work even in St st for 5 rnds. Bind off loosely.

INNER EARS

(make two)

Beg at tip with straight needles and B, cast on 1 st.
Row 1 (WS) Work (p1, k1, p1) into st—3 sts.
Row 2 and all RS rows Knit.
Row 3 P1, M1, p1, M1, p1—5 sts.
Row 5 P1, M1, p3, M1, p1—7 sts.
Rows 7, 11, 15 and 17 Purl.
Row 9 P1, M1, p5, M1, p1—9 sts.
Row 13 P1, M1, p7, M1, p1—11 sts.
Bind off loosely.

FINISHING

Open zipper. Center and pin dog applique on front of pillow, with lower edge of applique about 2"/5cm from zipper edge of pillow. Sew applique to pillow. Stuff snout lightly with fiberfill and sew to applique referring to photo for positioning. Attach eyes. Sew inner ears in place. Tie a small bow and sew at top of head.

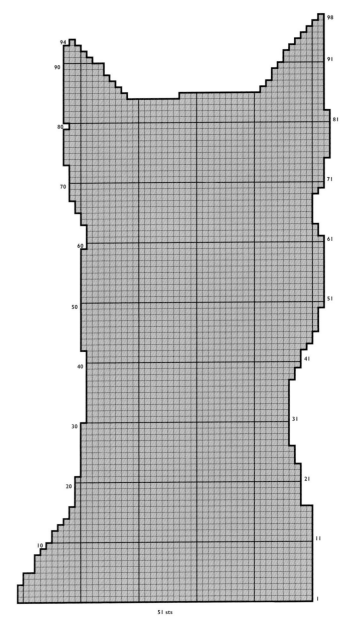

51 sts

59

■■■□

BLACK AND WHITE CAT PILLOW

KNITTED MEASUREMENTS
■ Approx 16"/40.5cm square

MATERIALS
■ 6 1¾oz/50g balls (each approx 109yd/100m) of Naturally NZ *Merino et Soie* 10-ply(wool/silk) in #101 grey (MC) ■

■ 1 1¾oz/50g ball (approx 77yd/70m) of S.R. Kertzer, Ltd., *Ranee* (or Naturally *Imagine*) (polymide/polyester) in #10 black (A) ■

■ 1 1¾oz/50g ball (approx 131yd/120m) of Naturally NZ *Sensation* (wool/angora) in #300 white (B) ■

■ Small amount black yarn

■ One pair size 6 (4mm) needles, *or size to obtain gauge*

■ One set (4) size 6 (4mm) double-pointed needles (dpn)

■ Six stitch markers

■ Small amount polyester fiberfill

■ 16"/40.5cm square pillow form

■ 12"/30.5cm grey zipper

■ Tapestry needle

■ One pair 1"/25mm cat's eyes

■ Transparent fishing line for whiskers

■ Ribbon or tulle for collar

■ Small charm

GAUGE
20 sts and 26 rows to 4"/10cm over pat st using size 6 (4mm) needles.
Take time to check gauge.

PILLOW COVER
Work as for black cat on page 52.

APPLIQUE
With straight needles and A, cast on 52 sts. Following notes for working chart as for black cat on page 53, work 92 rows of chart in St st, following chart for shaping and color changes. On row 69 of chart, work 11 sts, join 2nd ball of yarn, bind off 5 sts, work to end. Working both sides at once, complete chart.

SNOUT
With B, work as for black cat on page 53.

FINISHING
Finish as for black cat on page 53, except replace the collar with ribbon (see photo) and sew in place rather than gluing it. Sew charm to ribbon as shown.

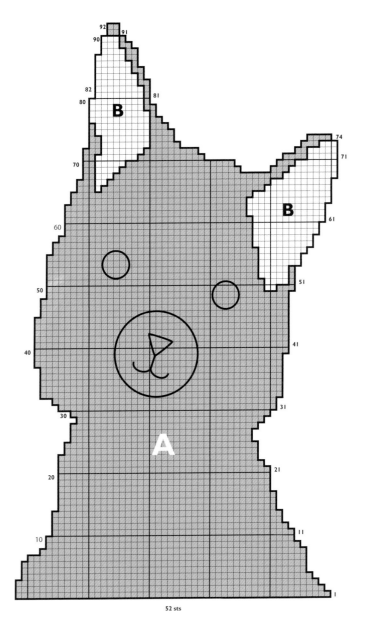

92 91
90
82 81
80
B
70
60
B
61
50
51
41
40
31
30
A
21
20
11
10
71 74
1

52 sts

61

DOG BOOTIES
Mutt mittens

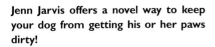

Jenn Jarvis offers a novel way to keep your dog from getting his or her paws dirty!

SIZE

Instructions are written for Dog's size Small/Medium.

KNITTED MEASUREMENTS

■ Sole 3"/7.5cm (before felting)

MATERIALS

■ 1¾oz/50g balls (each approx 55yd/50m) of Classic Elite Yarns *Paintbox* (wool) in #6889 matisse's landscape ⑤
■ One set (4) size 11 (8mm) double-pointed needles (dpn) *or size to obtain gauge*
■ One package ⅝"/15mm-wide Velcro
■ Sewing needle
■ Sewing thread
■ Tapestry needle

GAUGE

11 sts and 14 rows to 4"/10cm over St st using size 11 (8mm) dpn.
Take time to check gauge.

BOOTIE

Sole
Cast on 5 sts.
Row 1 K across, cast on 2 sts at end—7 sts.
Row 2 P across, cast on 2 sts at end—9 sts.
Rows 3—10 Work in St st.
Row 11 Bind off 2 sts, k across.
Row 12 Bind off 2 sts, p across.

Side of bootie
Row 1 K across, pick up and k 12 sts along left side and front of bootie, cast on 1 st—18 sts. Turn and p across all sts. Pick up and p 12 sts along right side and front of bootie, cast on 1 st—31 sts.
Rows 2 and 3 Turn and work across all sts in St st for 2 rows.
Row 4 K to last 3 sts, k2tog, k1.
Row 5 P to last 3 sts, p2tog tbl, p1.
Rows 6—9 Rep rows 4 and 5 twice more—25 sts.
Rows 10 and 11 Work 2 rows in St st.
Row 12 K across, cast on 2 sts.
Row 13 P across, cast on 2 sts.
Rows 14 and 15 Rep rows 12 and 13 once more—33 sts.
Rows 16—18 Work 3 rows in St st.
Row 19 Bind off first 19 sts, p to end of row. Bind off rem sts.

FINISHING

Sew front seam from sole to row 10. Weave in ends.

Felting
Felt the booties in the washing machine with a towel, detergent, hot water, and regular wash cycle. You should not be able to see individual stitches when the felting is complete. If you can, run the booties through the wash and rinse cycle again. It may take 3 times to get the booties to felt if your water is not very hot. You can add boiling water to the wash cycle to add heat, also.

Cut one ½"/1.3cm pieces of Velcro for each bootie. Sew on bootie so that flaps overlap.

FAIR ISLE DOG BED

See spot sleep

This fun, colorful pattern by Kate Jackson gives your dog a cozy, warm place to catch some Zs.

KNITTED MEASUREMENTS
▧ 18 x 30 x 3"/45.5 x 76 x 7.5cm

MATERIALS
▧ 2 3½oz/100g balls (each approx 220yd/201m) of Nashua Handknits Westminster Fibers *Focus Worsted* (wool/alpaca) in #2055 carmine (A) ▧
▧ 1 ball each in #1256 soft sage (B), #3864 bud green (C), #3686 carolina (D) and #410 espresso (E)
▧ Size 7 (4.5mm) circular knitting needle, 36"/91.5cm long *or size to obtain gauge*
▧ Tapestry needle
▧ 3"/7.5cm-thick foam, cut to size 18 x 30"/45.5 x 76cm
▧ ½yd/.5m 60"/151.5cm-wide red canvas for bottom
▧ Sewing thread
▧ Sewing machine

GAUGE
23 sts and 25 rows to 4"/10cm over St st and chart pat using size 7 (4.5mm) needle. *Take time to check gauge.*

Note
Circular knitting needle is used to accommodate large amount of sts.

TOP OF BED
With A, cast on 109 sts. Do not join. Work in St st for 2 rows.
Beg chart on row 1, work 36-st rep 3times across row, end with st 37. Work even through row 52, then rep rows 1–52 twice more, then rows 1–35 once (4 paw stripes and 3 bone stripes).
With A, work in St st for 2 rows. Bind off.

SIDE PIECE
With C, cast on 450 sts. Do not join. Work in St st in stripe pat as foll: 4 rows C, 4 rows A, 1 row D, 2 rows E, 1 row D, 4 rows A and 4 rows C. Bind off.

FINISHING
Weave in ends. Sew side edges of side piece tog. Sew this piece around the edge of the top, making sure to ease carefully while sewing.
On a sewing machine, baste along the bottom edge of each side about ⅛"/.3cm in to help the easing between knit fabric and canvas.
Cut 2 pieces of canvas 18 x 19"/45.5 x 48cm. Hem 1"/2.5cm under on one side of each piece to make two 18"/45.5cm squares.

Align these pieces, hem together, with a 4"/10cm overlap and baste the edges along the overlap. Pin the bottom to the sides, right sides together, and sew with a ¼"/.6cm seam allowance. This will work best with the canvas on the bottom and the knit fabric on top. Turn the entire piece with right side out and insert the piece of foam.

Gently steam the finished piece to smooth your stitches and seams.

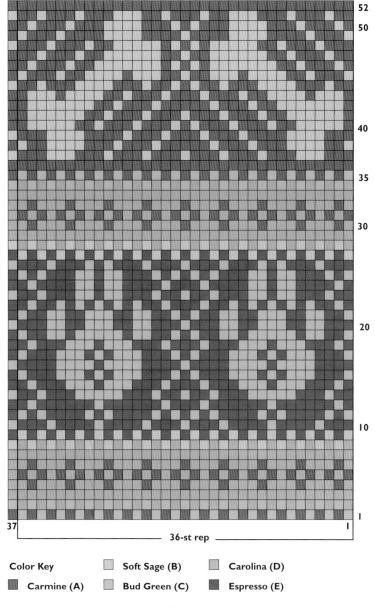

52
50

40

35

30

20

10

1

37

36-st rep

1

Color Key

Soft Sage (B)

Carolina (D)

Carmine (A)

Bud Green (C)

Espresso (E)

■■■□□

Cecelia Madison's playful design will provide your cat with hours of fun...not to mention a chance to work off some of that cat food!

KNITTED MEASUREMENTS
■ Approx 4 x 5"/10 x 12.5cm (before felting)
■ Approx 2½ x 3½"/7 x 9.5cm (after felting)

MATERIALS
■ 4oz/113g ea approx Brown Sheep Company *Lamb's Pride* Worsted (wool/mohair) for each fish in #M110 orange you glad, #M105 pink, #M57 brite blue or #M100 supreme purple per fish (4)
■ One set (5) size 11 (8mm) double-pointed needles (dpn) *or size to obtain gauge*
■ Stitch holder
■ Stitch marker
■ Tapestry needle
■ Catnip
■ Polyester fiberfill
■ Sewing needle
■ Thread to match yarn

GAUGE
Approx 12 sts and 24 rows to 4"/10cm over garter st using size 11 (8mm) dpn (before felting).

Take time to check gauge.

Notes
1 Fish body is worked in the round beginning at the head, and then divided for tail.
2 The stitch counts will be easier to track if the work is divided onto 4 double-pointed needles.

CATNIP TOY
Cast on 12 sts, dividing evenly onto 4 dpn. Taking care not to twist sts, join and pm for beg of rnds. P 1 rnd.

Shape head
Rnd 1 [Sl 1 wyib, k into the front and back of the next st, k3, k into the front and back of the next st] twice—16 sts.
Rnds 2, 4 and 6 Purl.
Rnd 3 [Sl 1 wyib, k into the front and back of the next st, k5, k into the front and back of the next st] twice—20 sts.
Rnd 5 [Sl 1 wyib, k into the front and back of the next st, k7, k into the front and back of the next st] twice—24 sts.

Main body
Rnds 7, 9, 11 and 13 [Sl 1 wyib, k11] twice.
Rnds 8, 10, 12 and 14 Purl.
Shape body
Rnd 15 [Sl 1 wyib, k2tog, k7, ssk] twice—20 sts.
Rnds 16, 18 and 20 Purl.
Rnd 17 [Sl 1 wyib, k2tog, k5, ssk]

twice—16 sts.

Rnd 19 [Sl 1 wyib, k2tog, k3, ssk] twice—12 sts.

Tail

Row 1 K into front and back of first st, k4, k into the front and back of the next st, turn—8 sts. Place rem 6 sts on holder.

Rows 2, 4 and 6 Knit.

Row 3 K into front and back of first st, k6, k into the front and back of the last st—10 sts.

Row 5 K into front and back of first st, k8, k into the front and back of the last st—12 sts.

Row 7 K into front and back of first st, k10, k into the front and back of the last st —14 sts.

Row 8 Bind off.

Place rem 6 sts on holder back to dpn.

Rejoin yarn and work rows 1–8.

Sew head closed. Weave in loose ends.

Felting

Put fish in zippered pillowcase. Add to washing machine with towels, jeans, or tennis balls for added friction. Use the lowest water level, the hottest water setting, and a small amount of soap. Set machine to agitate and check progress every 5–10 minutes. Turn fish inside out for some of the time. Reset the machine to agitate if more time is needed. Do not allow machine to enter spin cycle, as this will cause a permanent crease in the fish. When the wool is matted, rinse fish. Roll it in a towel and squeeze out as much water as possible. Pinch fish at base of tail with one hand and pull at each corner of the tail to flare it. Gently pull body into a rounded shape. Stuff body of fish with a mix of catnip and fiberfill. Sew closed tightly across base of tail with either leftover yarn or thread.

CAT TOY

Chase this!

Ava Green's colorful ball on a string, with handle, makes for tons of fun, healthy one-on-one communication with your cat.

KNITTED MEASUREMENTS

- Ball 3½"/9cm diameter
- Hanger/string 30"/76cm long

MATERIALS

- 1 1¾oz/50g ball (approx 88yd/81m) of Muench/GGH *Savanna Colors* (alpaca/linen/wool/nylon) #102 yellow multi ⬛
- One pair size 8 (5mm) knitting needles *or size to obtain gauge*
- Two size 7 (4.5mm) double-pointed needles (dpn)
- Catnip
- Polyester fiberfill
- One ¾"/19mm jingle bell
- Ruler
- Scissors

GAUGE

16 sts and 20 rows to 4"/10cm over St st using size 8 (5mm) needles.
Take time to check gauge.

SPECIAL ABBREVIATION

wrap & turn (w&t)
Knit side
1 Wyib, sl next st purlwise.
2 Move yarn between the needles to the front of work.
3 Sl the same st back to LH needle. Turn work, bring yarn to the purl side between needles. One st is wrapped, you are ready to work next row. When short rows are completed, the wraps must be hidden. Work to just before wrapped st, insert RH needle under the wrap and knitwise into the wrapped st, k them tog.

Purl side
1 Wyif, sl next st purlwise.
2 Move yarn between the needles to the back of work.
3 Sl the same st back to LH needle. Turn work, bring yarn to the purl side between needles. One st is wrapped, you are ready to work next row. When short rows are completed, the wraps must be hidden. Work to just before wrapped st, insert RH needle from behind into the back loop of the wrap and place it on the LH needle. Purl it tog with the st on the LH needle.

BALL

With straight needles, cast on 16 sts.

Row 1 P16.

Row 2 K14, w&t.

Row 3 P11, w&t.

Row 4 K9, w&t.

Row 5 P7, w&t.

Row 6 K5, w&t.

Row 7 P to the end, working the wraps with the sts.

Row 8 K to the end, working the wraps with the sts.

Row 9 P14, w&t.

Row 10 K11, w&t.

Row 11 P9, w&t.

Row 12 K7, w&t.

Row 13 P5, w&t.

Row 14 K to the end, working the wraps with the sts.

Row 15 P to the end, working the wraps with the sts.

Rep rows 2–15 three times more.

Bind off, leaving 18"/45.5cm tail. Thread the yarn needle with the yarn tail. Run the yarn through the sts on the bound-off edge and gather the edge closed. Fasten the yarn and weave in the ends.

I-CORD HANGER

With dpn, cast on 5 sts.

Work I-cord for 32"/81cm as foll: *K5, do not turn, slide sts back to opposite end of needle, pull yarn across back; rep from *. Bind off, leaving an 18"/45.5cm tail.

FINISHING

Mark the cord 8"/20.5cm from the bound off end. Fold the end to the marker and stitch to the cord to make a loop. Stitch the other end to the top of the ball where the edge was gathered. Stuff the ball with polyester fiberfill and catnip, placing jingle bell in the middle. Use yarn to gather the bottom edge tightly closed. Fasten off. Weave in and trim the ends of the yarn.

TARTAN CAPE
Preppy puppy

■■ ■■ ■■ ▭

Even a mutt looks like a show dog in this classy creation by Pauline Schultz.

KNITTED MEASUREMENTS
■ Approx 35 x 21"/89 x 53.5cm

MATERIALS
■ 5oz/141g skein (approx 278yd/254m) of Coats & Clark *Red Heart Super Saver* (acrylic) each in #0334 buff (A), #0376 burgundy (B) and #0387 soft navy (C) 🄸
■ Size 8 (5mm) circular knitting needle, 24"/61cm long *or size to obtain gauge*
■ Scrap yarn
■ Crochet hook size H/8(5mm)
■ Two size 8 (5mm) double-pointed needles (dpn)
■ Bobbins
■ Coordinating color fabric for lining
■ Two size 10 snaps

GAUGE
16 sts and 24 rows to 4"/10 cm in plaid pattern over St st
Take time to check gauge.

STITCH PATTERNS
Slip Rib
(multiple of 2 sts plus 1)
Row 1 (RS) K1, *k1, p1; rep from * to end.
Row 2 P1, *sl 1 wyif, p1; rep from * to end.
Rep rows 1 and 2 for slip rib.

PROVISIONAL CAST-ON
1 Using waste yarn of a similar weight to the project yarn, chain 144. Cut a tail and pull the tail through the last chain.
2 Using the circular needles and working yarn, pick up one stitch through the "purl bumps" on the back of each crochet chain. Be careful not to split the waste yarn, as this makes it difficult to pull out the crochet chain at the end.
3 Work pattern as instructed.
4 To remove waste chain, pull out the tail from the last crochet stitch. Gently and slowly pull on the tail to unravel the crochet stitches, carefully placing each released knit stitch on a needle.

I-CORDS
Method 1
*K2C, [k 1 C and 1 A] tog tbl, do not turn, sl these 3 sts back to opposite end of needle; rep from *.
Method 11
Work same as method 1 but pick up bar(s) between middle and edge sts.

Notes
1 Use a separate bobbin of yarn for each color change.
2 When changing colors, twist yarn on WS to prevent holes.

PLAID PATTERN
Worked in St st over 144 sts

Rows 1, 3, 5, 7 (RS)K 3A, *12B, 2A; rep from *, end 3A.

Row 2 and all WS rows Purl across, working the colors as established on previous RS row.

Rows 9, 11, 13, 15 K 3A, *6C, 6B, 2A, 6B, 6C, 2A; rep from *, end 6C, 3A.

Row 17 Knit across with A.

Rows 19, 21, 23, 25 K 3A, *6C, 6B, 2A, 6B, 6C, 2A; rep from *, end 6C, 3A.

Rows 27, 29, 31, 33 K 3A, *12B, 2A; rep from *, end 3A.

Row 35 Knit across with A.

Rows 37, 39, 41, 43 K 3A, *12B, 2A; rep from *, end 3A.

Rows 45, 47, 49, 51 K 3A, *6B, 6C, 2A, 6C, 6B, 2A; rep from *, end 3A.

Row 53 Knit across with A.

Rows 55, 57, 59, 61 K 3A, *6B, 6C, 2A, 6C, 6B, 2A; rep from *, end 3A.

Row 63, 65, 67, 69 K 3A, *12B, 2A; rep from *, end 3A.

71 Knit across with A.

Row 72 Purl across with A.

Repeat rows 1–72 for Plaid pattern.

Using provisional cast-on technique and A, cast on 144 sts.

Shape back corners

With A, knit 1 row, purl 1 row.

Work row 1 of plaid pattern as follows: K3A, sl next 12 sts to LH needle, attach sep bobbin of A and k 2A, [k 12B, k2A] across row to last 15 sts, k 4B, turn.

Next row Purl across, following colors as established, p 4B, turn. Continue to work plaid pattern AT SAME TIME, work 4 more sts in pat at end of the next 3 rows, then work 7 more sts at the end of next 2 rows–all 144 sts are worked. Work rows 1–72 once, then rows 1–35 once more.

Shape neck and front corners

Left side

Next row(WS)

Purl across 57 sts in row 36 of plaid pat, turn, k 57 for row 37. Cont in pat, working 2 less sts at the end of each WS row (neck edge) 4 times–49 sts.

Next row (RS) Work to last 6 sts, turn–43 sts. Cont in pat and work 3 sts less at the end of each RS row 3 times more, 2 sts less at the end of each WS row 3 times more–28 sts. Sl 29 unworked sts at end of RS row to RH needle, turn, join A and p across row.

Right side

Work in plaid pat and dec in same manner as for left side by working 2 less sts at the end of RS rows (neck edge) and then 3 less sts at the end of WS rows. When all decs have been worked, sl 28 worked RS sts to RH needle with unworked sts and knit across with A. Purl 1 row, knit one row across 144 sts with A.

With dpn and C, cast on 3 sts. P 1 row.

Working along front edge raw sts, work method I of I-cord, then work method II along side; return provisional cast on sts to circular needle and work method I, end with method II along rem side. Sew i-cord ends tog.

CHEST STRAP

With C, cast on 7 sts. Work in rib pat for 14"/35.5cm. Bind off in rib pat.

UNDERBODY STRAP

Work as for chest strap for 16"/40.5cm. Bind off.

FINISHING

Wash and block knitted piece (and fabric if necessary). Lay knitted piece on WS of fabric and trace around with pencil. Cut fabric to size, with extra ½" of fabric all around for hem. Lay fabric and knitted piece with WS tog. Pin in place, turning over ½"/1.3cm hem, sl st around edge. Along center back, tack to knitted piece invisibly "in the ditch" between 2 "A" sts. Sew chest strap to front inside of piece approx 9"/23cm from center back, securing. Attach the underbody strap approx 10"/25.5cm in from side edge and 6"/15cm from center back by sewing one end to the coat and using the snaps to secure the other end.

Micki Hair has created this cute, clever container for biscuits, vitamins and whatever else your furry friend might need.

KNITTED MEASUREMENTS

Finished size measures 9 x 12 x 4"/23 x 30.5 x 10cm

MATERIALS

▓ 4 5oz/140g skeins (each approx 236yd/212m) of Lion Brand *Lion Cotton* (cotton) in #100 white (MC) 🔵
▓ 1 skein each in #153 black (A) and #112 poppy red (B)
▓ One pair each size 6 and 7 (4 and 4.5mm) knitting needles or size to obtain gauge
▓ One set (4) size 7 (4.25mm) double-pointed needles (dpn)
▓ Stitch markers
▓ One package (8) ½"/13mm grommets
▓ Grommet setter
▓ Four black single hole plastic cord stoppers
▓ 1yd/1m black elastic cord
▓ ¼yd/.25m black elastic thread
▓ 1yd/1m of 1½"/38mm-wide black and white gingham ribbon
▓ One ¼"/6mm black button
▓ Contents of first aid kit: thermometer, antiseptic wipes, small plastic bottles for ear wash and peroxide, Neosporin, aspirin, nail clippers, tweezers, gauze, tape and feel good treat.

GAUGES

▓ 24 sts and 28 rows to 4"/10cm over rosette st using size 7 (4.5mm) needles.
▓ 20 sts and 28 rows to 4"/10cm over St st using size 7 (4.5mm) needles.
Take time to check gauge.

ROSETTE STITCH

Rows 1 and 3 (RS) Knit.
Row 2 (WS) *P2tog, leave on needle; k same 2 sts tog and sl from needle together; rep from * to end.
Row 4 P1, *p2tog, leave on needle, k same 2 sts tog and sl from needle together; rep from *, end p1.
Rep rows 1–4 for rosette stitch.

SEED STITCH

Row 1(RS) *K1, p1; rep from * to end.
Row 2 K the purl sts and P the knit sts.
Rep row 2 for seed st.

MATTRESS STITCH

With RS of knitting facing, use threaded needle to pick up one bar between first 2 sts on one piece, then corresponding bar plus the bar above it on the other piece. Rep this, remembering to pull thread to tighten, making an invisible seam.

OUTSIDE FRONT

With larger needles and MC, cast on 72 sts, placing markers on sts 30 and 42. Keeping each end st in selvage st (k every row), work even in rosette st until piece measures 5¼"/13.5cm from beg, ending with a WS row.

Next row (RS) Work buttonholes on sts 30 and 42 as follows: yo twice, k2tog. On following row, drop one loop of yo, work rem loop as st. Continue in rosette st until piece measures 9"/23cm from beg. Bind off.

OUTSIDE BACK WITH FLAP

With larger needles and MC, cast on 72 sts, placing markers on sts 30 and 42. Keeping each end st in selvage st, work even in rosette st until piece measures 12"/30.5cm from beg, ending with a WS row.

Next row (RS) Bind off 2 sts at beg of next 2 rows, work 4 rows even. Rep these 6 rows 5 times more—48 sts AT THE SAME TIME, when piece measures 14"/35.5cm, work buttonholes on marked sts on a RS row. Continue in rosette st until piece measures 15½"/39.5cm from beg. Bind off.

INSIDE FRONT

With larger needles and MC, cast on 60 sts. Keeping each end st in selvage st, work 2 rows in St st.

Next row (RS) Place markers on sts 6 & 17 (pocket 1), on sts 21 & 44 (pocket 2), and on sts 48 & 55 (pocket 3).

Work even until piece measures 4¾"/12cm from beg. On RS row, place markers on sts 8 & 15(pocket 4). Work even until piece measures 9"/23cm from beg. Bind off.

POCKETS

Note All pockets are worked as follows: with smaller needle and MC, pick up sts between markers, with larger needles work in St st for desired length. Work 2 rows of seed st. Bind off in seed st with A.

Pocket 1 Pick up the 12 sts between markers, work in St st until pocket measures 3½"/9cm. Finish as above.

Pocket 2 Pick up the 24 sts between markers and work in St st for 6¾"/17cm. Finish as above.

Pocket 3 Pick up the 8 sts between markers and work in St st for 7¼"/18.5cm. Finish as above.

Pocket 4 Pick up 8 sts between markers and work in St st for 2¾"/7cm. Finish as above.

INSIDE BACK WITH FLAP

Cast on 60 sts and work same as for inside front, placing markers on sts 6 & 27 (pocket 5), and on sts 31 & 55(pocket 6). Work even until piece measures

5¼"/13.5cm from beg, place markers on sts 10 & 23(pocket 7). When piece measures 7"/17.5cm, place markers on sts 36 & 55(pocket 8).

When piece measures 9"/23cm, change to seed st. Place markers on sts 30 & 42 for buttonholes. Work even until piece measures 12"/30cm from beg. Dec 1 st each side every RS row 11 times—38 sts.

Next row Work inside front pockets in same manner as before:

Pocket 5 Pick up the 22 sts between markers, work in St st until pocket measures 4½"/11.5cm. Finish as above.

Pocket 6 Pick up the 25 sts between markers, work in St st until pocket measures 6"/15cm. Finish as above.

Pocket 7 Pick up the 14 sts between markers, work in St st until pocket measures 2¼"/5.5cm. Finish as above.

Pocket 5 Pick up the 20 sts between markers, work in St st until pocket measures ½"/1.3cm. Finish as above.

FINISH POCKETS

Remove markers. Lay pockets flat on inside front and inside back with flap. With A, whip-stitch sides of each pocket in place. Sew down the center of the 3 large pockets, dividing into 2 pockets.

GUSSETS

(make 2)

With larger needles and MC, cast on 21 sts. Work even in seed st for 1"/2.5cm. Work buttonholes on sts 3, 8, 13, and 18. Continue in seed st until piece measures 20"/51cm. Rep buttonhole row on same sts. Work 1"/2.5cm more, making piece 21"/53.5cm total, and bind off in seed st.

KNITTED DOG BONE WITH CROSS

With smaller needles and 2 balls of A, cast on 2 sets of 3 sts each. In St st, work rows 1—4 of of chart on each set of sts, join and work rows 5—19. Bind off 3 sts each set. Work cross in duplicate st with B, then backstitch around cross to outline. Sew dog bone onto outside flap 3¼"/2cm above buttonholes.

FINISHING

Block all pieces by pinning to size and steaming. Weave in all ends. Sew button above smallest pocket on inside back with flap. Attach a small piece of black elastic thread to top of pocket to wrap around button. With scrap yarn, baste outside front to inside front, and outside back to inside back. Place gussets together, one on top of the other so buttonholes line up, baste together. Place markers on side edges of fronts and backs at 4"/10cm from the bottom. Using the mattress stitch, sew the bottom edge of inside front to the top gusset between markers. Sew the outside front to the bottom gusset in the same manner, being sure to have ends of gussets meeting and buttonholes aligned. Stitch the inside back with flap to the top gusset in same manner, then stitch the outside back with flap to the bottom gusset respectively. Install grommets to all buttonholes, through both layers of knitting.

ATTACHED I-CORD TRIM

With dpn, cast on 3 sts. Sl sts back to opposite end of needle. With RS facing, begin at corner of right side gusset and back. *Pick up 1 edge st from both front and back—5 sts. K3tog (including 2 edge sts), k 2. Sl sts back to opposite end of needle. Rep from *, working across the top of the gusset, across the edge of the front of the bag, across the second gusset, then around the back of the bag and flap, ending at the first gusset. Bind off, stitch i-cord ends tog. Thread elastic cord through gusset eyelets and attach cord stoppers to inside of bag. Cinch to tighten. Weave ribbon through front eyelets and tie bow to close.

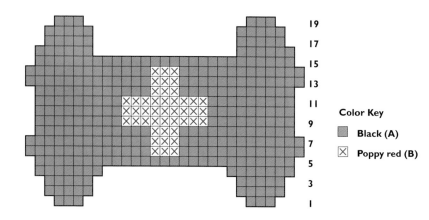

Color Key

- ▢ Black (A)
- ☒ Poppy red (B)

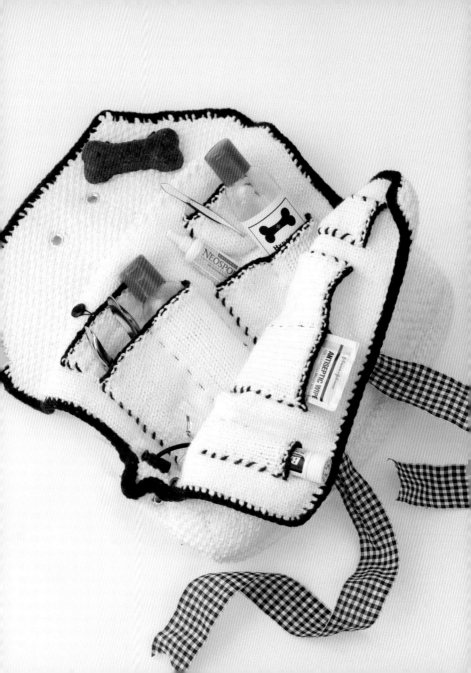

HORSESHOE CABLE

Joker's wild

Pompons adorn this cabled sweater by Gayle Bunn.

SIZE

Instructions are written for Dog's size Small.

KNITTED MEASUREMENTS

▪ Chest 13"/33cm

▪ Length 14"/35.5cm (from collar to base of tail)

MATERIALS

▪ 2 1¾oz/50g balls (each approx 150yd/137m) of Plymouth Yarns *Encore DK* (acrylic/wool) in #1384 purple (MC) (3)

▪ 1 ball in #1385 pink (CC)

▪ One pair size 6 (4mm) knitting needles *or size to obtain gauge*

▪ One set (4) size 6 (4mm) double-pointed needles (dpn)

▪ Cable needle

▪ Stitch holder

▪ Stitch marker

▪ Bobbins

GAUGE

22 sts and 30 rows to 4"/10 cm over St st using size 6 (4mm) needles.

Take time to check gauge.

STITCH GLOSSARY

C8B Sl next 4 sts onto cable needle and hold to back of work, k4, then k4 from cable needle.

C8F Sl next 4 sts onto cable needle and hold to front of work, k4, then k4 from cable needle.

CABLE PANEL

(multiple of 23 sts plus 7)

Row 1 (RS) *P7, C8B, C8F; rep from *, end p7.

Row 2 and all WS rows *K7, p16; rep from *, end k7.

Rows 3, 5, 7, 9 and 11 *P7, k16; rep from *, end p7.

Row 12 *K7, p16; rep from *, end k7.

Rep rows 1–12 for cable panel.

COAT

With MC and straight needles, cast on 53 sts loosely.

Row 1 (RS) K1, *p1, k1; rep from * to end.

Row 2 P1, *k1, p1; rep from * to end.

Rep these 2 rows for k1, p1 ribbing for 1¼"/3cm, ending with row 2 and inc 3 sts evenly across—56 sts.

Body

Row 1 (RS) K13, work row 21 of cable panel over next 30 sts, k13.

Row 2 P13, work row 2 of cable panel across next 30 sts, p13.

Working in pat as established, inc 1 st each end of next 6 rows, then every RS row 11 times, working inc sts into cable pat—90 sts. Work 5 rows even.

Divide for legs

Next row (RS) P7, join second ball of yarn and bind off next 6 sts, work across to last 13 sts, join third ball of yarn and bind off next 6 sts, p to end of row.

Working these 3 sections at same time, cont in pat until 1½"/4cm from bound off sts, ending with a WS row.

Joining row (RS) P7, cast on 6 sts, work across 64 sts, cast on 6 sts, p to end of row—90 sts.

Cont even until work measures 9½"/24cm above ribbing, ending with a WS row. Place a marker at each end of last row.

Back shaping Bind off 4 sts beg next 2 rows—82 sts.

Dec 1 st at beg of next 18 rows–64 sts. Sl these sts to holder.

Notes

1 Work neck edging with separate bobbins of yarn for each section of color.

2 Carry yarns along RS rows, collar will be folded over.

Neck edging With WS facing, [with MC, pick up and k9 sts along cast-on edge of ribbing, with CC, pick up and k9 sts along cast-on edge of neckband] 3 times—54 sts.

Knit 7 rows in colors as established.

Shape points

Row 1(WS) Beg with first point, ssk, k5, k2tog–7 sts; turn and work separately on this point.

Row 2 and all WS rows Knit.

Row 3 Ssk, k3, k2tog.

Row 5 Ssk, k1, k2tog.

Row 7 Sl 1, k2tog, psso. Fasten off.

Rep rows 1–7 across each of rem 5 points.

Leg edging

With RS facing, MC and dpns, pick up and k 30 sts evenly spaced around leg opening. Join and pm for beg of rnds. Work in garter st (k 1 rnd, p 1 rnd) for 5 rnds. Bind off purlwise.

Notes

1 Work back edging with separate bobbins of yarn for each section of color.

2 Carry yarns along WS rows.

Back edging

With RS facing, MC and straight needles, pick up and k15 sts along angled edge between marker and st holder, k sts from holder and dec 9 sts evenly across, pick up and k15 sts along angled edge to marker—85 sts. K 2 rows.

Bind off 15 sts at beg next 2 rows–55sts.

Row 1 (RS) With RS facing [with CC, k11, with MC, k11] twice, end with CC, k11. Knit 7 rows in colors as established.

Shape points

Row 1 Beg with first CC point, ssk, k7, k2tog; turn and work separately on this point.

Row 2 and all WS rows K.

Row 3 Ssk, k5, k2tog.

Row 5 Ssk, k3, k2tog.

Row 7 Ssk, k1, k2tog.

Row 9 Sl 1, k2tog, psso. Fasten off.

Rep rows 1–9 across each of remaining 4 points.

Sew center seam from neck edging to back edging. Make 3 pom-poms each with MC and CC. Attach to each point of neck edging as shown.

Three blind mice

■■ ■■ ▢ ▢

Ava Green's pattern is a sure bet to get those paws flying!

KNITTED MEASUREMENTS
■ 4"/10cm from head to start of tail (after felting)

MATERIALS
■ 1¾oz/50g of Rowan/Westminster Fibers *Harris DK* (wool) each in #3 sage, #11 sunset and #5 lavender **1**
■ 18"/4.5cm DMC Tapestry Wool in black for eyes
■ One pair size 9 (5.5mm) knitting needles
■ Darning needle
■ Polyester fiberfill or catnip for stuffing
■ Ruler
■ Scissors

GAUGE
Gauge is not important.

STITCH GLOSSARY
bobble Knit into the next stitch 5 times, turn, p5, turn, k5, turn, p5, turn, k the 5 stitches together.

Notes
1 The ears are bobbles.
2 The eyes are stitched after felting and before stuffing.

FELTED MOUSE CAT TOY
Cast on 24 sts.

Row 1 P across.
Row 2 K21, turn.
Row 3 Yo, p18, turn.
Row 4 Yo, k16, turn.
Row 5 Yo, p14, turn.
Row 6 Yo, k13, turn.
Row 7 Yo, p12, turn.
Row 8 Yo, k10, turn.
Row 9 Yo, p7, M1, p1, turn.
Row 10 Yo, k7, M1, k1, turn
Row 11 Yo, p3, [M1, p1] 5 times, turn.
Row 12 Yo, k10, turn.
Row 13 Yo, [p1, M1] 7 times, turn.
Row 14 Yo, k13, turn.
Row 15 Yo, p11, turn.
Row 16 Yo, k9, turn.
Row 17 Yo, p8, turn.
Row 18 Yo, k2, bobble, k1, bobble, k2, turn.
Row 19 Yo, p6, turn.
Row 20 Yo, k5, turn.
Row 21 Yo, p4, turn.
Row 22 Yo, k3, turn.
Row 23 Yo, p2, turn.
Row 24 Yo, work across the row knitting each yo tog with the st following it.
Row 25 Work across the row purling each yo tog with the st following it.
Row 26 K across.
Bind off all sts.

Tail
Hold the cast-on edge with the RS facing you. Counting from the right edge, attach the yarn in the 10th st. Pick up 1 st in the

10th, 11th, 12th, and 13th sts of the cast-on edge.

Work in St st for 7"/17.5cm. Bind off. Cut the yarn with a 15"/38cm tail.

ASSEMBLY

Thread the darning needle with the 15"/38 tail. Seam the long edge of the tail. Run the yarn tail through the cast-on edge of tail and pull tight. Fold cast-on edge with tail in center and sew tog to form tail end of mouse. Starting at the nose, fold mouse in half and sew bound-off edge tog for center seam, leaving a 1½"/4cm opening. Weave in all the ends.

FELTING

Felt the mouse in the washing machine with a towel, detergent, hot water, and the regular wash cycle. You should not be able to see individual stitches when the felting is complete. If you can, run the mouse through the wash and rinse cycle again. It may take 3 times to get the mouse to felt if your water is not very hot. You can add boiling water to the wash cycle to add heat, also.

EMBROIDERY

Thread the needle with the black tapestry wool. Make a small black X for an eye about ¼"/.5cm below each ear. Stuff the mouse with fiberfill and catnip. Sew the opening closed with yarn and darning needle.

DOG COAT
Canine couture

Your pooch will be the envy of the best-dressed dogs in your neighborhood in Gayle Bunn s stylish knit coat.

SIZE

Instructions are written for Dog's size Small.

KNITTED MEASUREMENTS
■ Chest 13"/33cm
■ Length 12"/30.5cm (from collar to base)

MATERIALS
■ 3 1¾oz/50g balls (each approx 76yd/70m) of Knit One, Crochet Too *Italian Ice* (cotton/linen/viscose) in #1279 candy (MC)
■ 1 ball in #651 teal (CC)
■ One pair size 10½ (6.5mm) knitting needles *or size to obtain gauge*
■ Size G/6 (4mm) crochet hook
■ Four sets of ¾"/2cm Coin Set Velcro Fasteners
■ Stitch markers

GAUGE
13 sts and 16 rows to 4"/10cm over St st using 2 strands of yarn held tog and size 10½ (6.5mm) needles.
Take time to check gauge.

Note

Use 2 strands of yarn held tog throughout.

BODY

With 2 strands of MC held tog, cast on 19 sts. Cont in St st, inc 1 st each end of next 6 rows, then following alt rows twice more—35 sts.

Work 7 rows even.

Dec 1 st each end of next and following 4th row—31 sts. Place first set of markers at each end of last row.

Work 7 rows even. Place second set of markers at each end of last row.

Inc 1 st each end of next row and following 4th rows twice more—37 sts.

Work 3 rows even.

Divide for neck

Next row (RS) Inc 1 st in first st, k11, join another 2 strands of MC and bind off center 13 sts, k to last st, inc 1 st in last st–13 sts each side. Working both sides at same time, dec 1 st at each neck edge on next 4 rows, then on following RS row— 8 sts each side.

Work 9 rows even. Bind off.

With 2 stands of MC held tog, cast on 8 sts. Cont in St st for 6"/15cm, ending with a WS row.

Shape end Bind off 4 sts beg next 2 RS rows.

Work as for strap A, ending with a RS, working bind offs at beg of WS rows.

With single strand of MC and crochet hook, work 1 row of sc around outer edge of body, and around straps leaving bound off ends of straps free.

With 2 strands of CC, work blanket st embroidery around outer edge of body and straps. Embroider flower with CC as shown using chain stitch. Sew shaped edge of straps in position between markers. Sew 2 sets of Velcro fasteners each on straps and neck extension.

RESOURCES

Write to the yarn companies listed below for purchasing and mail-order information.

BERROCO, INC.
P.O. Box 367
14 Elmdale Road
Uxbridge, MA 01569
www.berroco.com

BROWN SHEEP COMPANY
100662 County Road 16
Mitchell, NB 69357
www.brownsheep.com

CLASSIC ELITE YARNS
122 Western Avenue
Lowell, MA 01851
www.classiceliteyarns.com

COATS & CLARK
Two LakePointe Plaza
4135 South Stream Blvd.
Charlotte, NC 28217
www.coatsandclark.com

DALE OF NORWAY, INC.
4750 Shelburne Road
Shelburne, VT 05482
www.daleofnorway.com

FIBER TRENDS
315 Colorado Park Place
P.O. Box 7266
East Wenatchee, WA 98802
www.fibertrends.com

FILATURA DI CROSA
distributed by
Tahki•Stacy Charles, Inc.

GGH
distributed by
Muench Yarns

JAEGER
distributed by
Westminster Fibers

JCA
35 Scales Lane
Townsend, MA 01469
www.jcacrafts.com

KARABELLA YARNS
1201 Broadway
New York, NY 10001
www.karabellayarns.com

KNIT ONE, CROCHET TOO, INC.
91 Tandberg Trail, Unit 6
Windham, ME 04062
www.knitonecrochettoo.com

LANA GROSSA
distributed by
Unicorn Books & Crafts

LION BRAND YARN
34 West 15th Street
New York, NY 10011
www.lionbrand.com

MUENCH YARNS, INC.
1323 Scott Street
Petaluma, CA 94954-1135
www.myyarn.com

NASHUA HANDKNITS
distributed by
Westminster Fibers

PLYMOUTH YARN COMPANY
P.O. Box 28
Bristol, PA 19007
www.plymouthyarn.com

REYNOLDS
distributed by
JCA

ROWAN YARNS
4 Townsend West, Unit 8
Nashua, NH 03063
www.knitrowan.com

TAHKI•STACY CHARLES, INC.
70-30 80th Street
Building #36
Ridgewood, NY 11385
www.tahkistacycharles.com

TAHKI YARNS
distributed by
Tahki•Stacy Charles, Inc.

UNICORN BOOKS & CRAFTS
1338 Ross Street
Petaluma, CA 94954
www.unicornbooks.com

WESTMINSTER FIBERS
4 Townsend West, Unit 8
Nashua, NH 03063
www.westminsterfibers.com

Write to US resources for mail-order availability of yarns not listed.

THE OLD MILL KNITTING COMPANY, INC.
F.G. P.O. Box 81176
Ancaster, Ontario L9G 4X2
www.oldmillknitting.com

PATONS YARNS
320 Livingstone Avenue
South
Listowel, ON
Canada N4W 3H3
www.patonsyarns.com

S.R. KERTZER, LTD.
50 Trowers Road
Woodbridge, ON
Canada L4L 7K6
www.kertzer.com

UK RESOURCES

Not all yarns used in this book are available in the UK. For yarns not available, make a comparable substitute or contact the US manufacturer for purchasing and mail-order information.

DALE OF NORWAY AS
5721 Dalekvam
Norway
47 56 59 54 00

NATURALLY N2
15 Church Street
Mall Onehunga
Auckland, New Zealand
www.naturallyyarnsnz.com

ROWAN
Green Lane Mill
Holmfirth
HD9 2DX England
www.knitrowan.com

VOGUE KNITTING KNITS FOR PETS

Editorial Director
TRISHA MALCOLM

Art Director
CHI LING MOY

Executive Editor
CARLA S. SCOTT

Book Division Manager
ERICA SMITH

Graphic Designer
SHEENA T. PAUL

Instructions Editor
RITA GREENFEDER

Instructions Proofreader
PAT HARSTE

Associate Editor
ERIN WALSH

Yarn Editor
TANIS GRAY

Production Manager
DAVID JOINNIDES

Photography
JACK DEUTSCH STUDIO

Photo Stylist
LAURA MAFFEO

Copywriter
ALAN YOUNG

■

President,
Sixth&Spring Books
ART JOINNIDES